# John Milton

The portrait of Milton on the title page was made in 1670 (when he was 62 and blind) by William Faithorne for the frontispiece to Milton's *History of Britain*, 1670. (From the copy in the Huntington Library.)

# John Milton

### THE INNER LIFE

## by James Thorpe

THE HUNTINGTON LIBRARY

1983

Library of Congress Cataloging in Publication Data
    Thorpe, James. 1915-
    John Milton: the inner life.
    1. Milton, John, 1608-1674.
2. Poets, English—Early Modern, 1500-1700—
Biography.   I. Title.
PR3581.T49   1983   821'.4   83-12602
ISBN 0-87328-079-2

# Contents

# Preface

THERE IS AN INTIMATE and complex relation between a close understanding of a poem and a deep understanding of its maker. This book tries to explore that relation with respect to the writings and the nature of John Milton.

Milton tells us a great deal about himself, or at least about the way he saw himself. His contemporaries add many facts and opinions about the way they saw him. In all, a strong, consistent, and believable person appears, if we choose to seek him out. This is the person whose inner profile I try to sketch in this book. It isn't necessary to resort to speculation in order to apprehend a sense of the real person that Milton was, and it certainly isn't necessary to look for him in a maze of psychological inference.

Milton's poems reflect his nature, with elegance. Sometimes the reflection is clear, sometimes obscure, sometimes a trial for our powers of perception. The "inner life" of the title of this book is intended to refer equally to the inner life of the man and the inner life of his writings, which have a life of their own.

The "inner life," as I use the term, is meant to suggest that mysterious world of motives, drives, and action that takes place within. It is where we establish and come to terms with our values, with our drives, and with our sense of self-esteem. It is where we mediate with the world outside of our selves, with the world of other human beings and with the world of nature. It is where we face our most important crises and where we seek our ultimate guidance in resolving our crucial problems. These are the topics that I try to deal with in this book. I approach them through a consideration of what we know of Milton's nature and of his writings, and of the relation of the two.

There are two possibilities that I have thought about as ideals for this book. One is to come to a better appreciation of Milton's writings, individually and collectively. The other is to reach a

# John Milton

better understanding of Milton's nature: to feel that we know, with a sense of confidence, what kind of person Milton was. So far as these great ideals can be reached through the plan of this book, the two now seem to me to be achievable mainly together, the one through the other, the other through the one.

The presentation I offer about the inner life of Milton and his writings is developed in seven chapters, which treat the topics I have just mentioned. Since each of the chapters depends to some extent on all of those that have preceded it, I hope that readers who prefer to dip first into a later chapter will realize that some of my argument is missing. Each chapter offers a number of conclusions. All of these conclusions, taken together, make up the gist of the story I would like to tell about the inner life of Milton and his writings.

This book is intended for all who have an interest in John Milton or in the issues to which I have referred. I write, of course, to fellow students of Milton, my friends and colleagues, and I offer them what I believe to be a different way of thinking about Milton and his writings. I write, as well, to other readers of Milton in the hope that they will find refreshment here, and that they will be encouraged to read Milton again with increased pleasure and understanding. I write, in hope, to those who have not yet read Milton with attention; he can, I believe, give a rich reward to those who are open to new aesthetic and intellectual experiences.

Where it was relevant to discuss exemplary passages from Milton's poetry or his prose, I have intentionally chosen poems or passages that seem to me to be among his best, and his best known. Some of them may be so familiar that it is hard to read them again, but I hope that the effort will be undertaken. If the discussion is successful, I trust that the limits of familiarity can be broken and that the passages may gain some new meaning in a new context. I hope also that the poetry and the prose will be seen, through their integration here, as the work of one Milton, not of two Miltons or of many Miltons.

A word about why I have chosen not to comment on earlier criticism and scholarship. The array of writing about almost

# The Inner Life

every aspect of Milton is indeed impressive, and sometimes almost overwhelming. It is often interesting to see which works from the past a scholar or critic singles out as relevant to what he has tried to do. After careful thought, I have decided–contrary to my first inclination–not to indulge myself by selecting earlier work for mention. To have done so thoroughly would perhaps have doubled the length of this book, and I doubt that the benefits would have been very great to anyone. All work has its particular dependencies, and students of Milton will readily perceive which work I have built on and that with which I have ventured to disagree. I express my profound gratitude to that multitude of scholars and critics of our own time–who must, to my regret, remain unnamed here–whose work has made such a vast contribution to our current understanding of Milton and (incidentally) to my personal education.

I have succeeded in resisting one other impulse: to try to demolish some of the myths about Milton. He has been a controversial figure from the beginning, and he has inflamed passions which the witty and the ill-tempered have turned into beguiling myths. That Milton was a tyrannical husband and father. That he was a sour and disagreeable man. That he was a bloodthirsty kingkiller. That he was a surly republican. That he was rigid and self-righteous. And so on and so forth. Even in our own time, uninformed popular writers have kept the old myths alive and created new ones.

I once thought that I could dispose of the hundred and one myths in an appendix. But good sense at last prevailed. I realized that these myths, being without foundation in fact, should be put aside as essentially irrelevant, however provoking they are to students of Milton. (Or, perhaps, be left for someone else to deal with.) For a reliable account of the known facts of the life of Milton, we have the comprehensive modern biography by William Riley Parker. (Some of his emphases and specific interpretations are inadequate, I think, but that is another matter; his book does succeed in giving a fair and balanced general understanding of its subject.) Students of Milton can distinguish between the myths and the facts. I hope that other readers will be willing to set aside their preconceptions unless they have satisfied themselves of the validity of those ideas by looking at the supporting evidence.

Several books are referred to frequently in the text by a short title:

*Prose. Complete Prose Works of John Milton*, Don M. Wolfe, general editor (New Haven: Yale University Press, 1953-82). I quote Milton's prose from and give references to this edition.

*Works. The Works of John Milton*, Frank Allen Patterson, general editor (New York: Columbia University Press, 1931-38). I use this edition for a few passages not available in *Prose*.

*Hughes. John Milton: Complete Poems and Major Prose*, ed. Merritt Y. Hughes (New York: The Odyssey Press, 1957 and later editions). I quote Milton's poems and some incidental passages from this edition because it still seems to be the most conveniently available one that offers reliable texts.

*Parker.* William Riley Parker, *Milton: A Biography* (Oxford: Clarendon Press, 1968).

I wish to thank, in particular, three friends and Milton scholars who generously read my manuscript. They are Joseph A. Wittreich, Jr., Roland Mushat Frye, and John M. Steadman. Their comments and suggestions helped me very much in improving what I had first written.

JAMES THORPE
*The Huntington Library*

# John Milton

# Chapter I
## The Sense of the Self
### THE INFORMING VALUES

———————— ❦❧❦❧ ————————

OUR IDEALS CREATE our personal form. The central values which constitute our ideals give us our sense of what we are, or what we like to think we are. Mostly we choose high values, but high values can rarely be fully achieved. Sometimes we are forced to twist away from them to find a more comfortable position to live in.

The values that seem to me to have been of the greatest importance to Milton have to do with three vast topics that dominated his inner life. First, his sense of his relationship to God. Second, his sense of his mission as a poet. And third, his sense of virtue. High values, noble ideals, difficult to attain. I would like to explore each of them to try to see what they meant to him. And, more important, how they shaped his life and his writings.

### I

For Milton, God was the central fact of life. He felt that God was his personal creator, and that the breath of his maker was always within him. All of his abilities, whatever they might be, were, he thought, gifts of God. The inspiration of God enabled him, he believed, to see what would otherwise have been invisible to mortal sight, to understand what would otherwise have been unknowable, and to write when he would otherwise have been mute. Milton gave heartfelt thanks to God for his achievements. He accepted misfortune—of which he had, with Job, much more than a normal share—as the working out of the divine

3

will, in which he acquiesced without grumbling; and in his times of trouble God gave him, he felt, comfort and support. These beliefs were the foundations on which Milton built his life.

This thumbnail sketch perhaps resembles the beginning of a saint's life, like Isaak Walton setting the stage for his reverential account of the life of George Herbert. Let me say, at the outset, that I do not think that Milton was a saint in the ways I understand that term. He was a literary genius, to be sure—which is why most of us are interested in him—and he was an exceedingly complex human being. (I hope that we can recognize, fairly, at least some of his special complexities.) But he had a full measure of weaknesses, and failings, and shortcomings; some of them were, in fact, his way of adjusting himself to his sense of the nature and role of God in his life.

For most of us today, it is easier to understand the tenets of Milton's doctrinal position than it is to respond fully to his personal sense of God. We talk and write a great deal about Milton's theology, but we are mostly silent about his sense of God, even though that sense may be very much more important in any deeply personal way, with whatever contingencies the deeply personal has in the life of art as well as in the art of living.

Short cuts toward understanding are beset by hazards. We mislead ourselves if we translate Milton's sense of God into such modern stereotypes as the figure of a Bible-quoting evangelist or a pious church-going Christian intent on saving his or her or your soul.

A further difficulty is that hardly anyone now believes all—or even most—of the complicated set of doctrines which made up Milton's special form of Christian faith. I do not agree (with T. S. Eliot, or C. S. Lewis, or with Coleridge before them) that it is necessary to share an author's religious (or other) convictions in order to understand his writings. Some of the most illuminating work on Milton in the last generation has been done by scholars whose personal convictions are (I understand) far removed from those which Milton had. I do think that an act of historical reconstruction is always necessary, and that is extraordinarily difficult in the case of Milton.

To begin with, it is worth reviewing a small sampling of Milton's self-revelations on his sense of God. Milton was remarkably open whenever he talked about himself, and he was always scrupulously honest (sometimes a little painfully so) in setting forth his convictions. He was given to self-examination, but not to morbid introspection. His remarks about God are mostly familiar, but we know them in a different context—as part of an invocation to a book of *Paradise Lost*, for example, where they are a part of our experience of that poem. In the context of Milton's sense of God, they may seem new once again and freshen our understanding. A few samples as reminders.

Even as a student, Milton had in mind his concern for the breath of immortal divinity in each person, including himself. In the Oration to his Seventh Prolusion, he tells his fellow students:

> It is, I think, a belief familiar and generally accepted that the great Creator of the world, while constituting all else fleeting and perishable, infused into man, besides what was mortal, a certain divine spirit, a part of Himself, as it were, which is immortal, imperishable, and exempt from death and extinction. After wandering about upon the earth for some time, like some heavenly visitant, in holiness and righteousness, this spirit was to take its flight upward to the heaven whence it had come and to return once more to the abode and home which was its birthright. It follows that nothing can be reckoned as a cause of our happiness which does not somehow take into account both that everlasting life and our ordinary life here on earth. (*Prose*, I, 291)

This "certain divine spirit" within him, which he later called "that divine particle of Gods breathing, the soul,"[1] was his permanent and indissoluble bond with God. It was a relationship

---

1. *Reason of Church-Government*, *Prose*, I, 848. Man "is both the image and glory of God" (*Apology Against a Pamphlet*, *Prose*, I, 892).

that carried heavy responsibilities, however; even as early as Sonnet VII ("How soon hath time," about 1632), Milton felt himself to be "ever in my great task-Master's eye." The idea of God as a personal taskmaster, overseeing a man suffering from the sin of Adam, imbued Milton for the rest of his life.

The classic statement of what Milton felt his personal obligation to be in living up to his relationship with God appears in *Of Education*. I believe that this passage is most valued for the balance of its rhetoric, or its supposed summation of a medieval point of view, or for the harmony of its diction. The statement is, in fact, a sincere, open, moving, personal testament: it tells what Milton himself wanted to learn to do in his life, and what he wanted to be able to achieve:

> The end then of learning is to repair the ruins of our first parents by regaining to know God aright, and out of that knowledge to love him, to imitate him, to be like him, as we may the neerest by possessing our souls of true vertue, which being united to the heavenly grace of faith makes up the highest perfection. (*Prose*, II, 366-67)[2]

Milton felt that God specially favored him, and he frequently expressed his thanks to God, as in this passage from *Defence of Himself*:

> Singular indeed is the favor of God toward me, that He has called me above all others to the defence of liberty, a cause which has been so bravely vindicated; and I confess that this favor I have acknowledged (nor should it ever go unacknowledged) and that I took thence the noble matter of my exordium, which, as I think, is in no way blameworthy. (*Prose*, IV, 735)[3]

2. The opening sentence of the essay is also worth remembering in this connection: "*Master Hartlib*, I am long since perswaded, that to say, or doe ought worth memory, and imitation, no purpose or respect should sooner move us, then simply the love of God, and of mankinde."

3. The *Second Defence* is rich in such expressions. Here are several examples from the early pages: "In the whole life and estate of man the first duty is to be

# The Inner Life

Except for the troubled, it is easier to accept gifts than misfortunes. But when calamities struck Milton, he received them as the will of God. Here, in the *Second Defence*, he is speaking of his blindness:

> I know and recognize in the most momentous affairs his fatherly mercy and kindness towards me, and especially in this fact, that with his consolation strengthening my spirit I bow to his divine will, dwelling more often on what he has bestowed on me than on what he has denied. (*Prose*, IV, 589)

Milton goes on to express the conviction that, on account of weakness, "there is hope that in this way I may approach more closely the mercy and protection of the Father Almighty" and thus travel the road from weakness "to the greatest strength" (589). He felt that "in my shadows the light of the divine countenance may shine forth all the more clearly. For then I shall be at once the weakest and the strongest, at the same time blind and most keen in vision. By this infirmity may I be perfected, by this completed. So in this darkness, may I be clothed in light" (590).

These are indeed noble words, and the more noble for being (as I believe) absolutely sincere. What we have come to consider among the noblest words of all, however, are embodied in the great invocations to *Paradise Lost* and *Paradise Regained*. All of them are addressed to the spirit of God, under one name or

---

grateful to God and mindful of his blessings, and to offer particular and solemn thanks without delay when his benefits have exceeded hope and prayer" (*Prose*, IV, 548). "In the belief that such great blessings come from on high and that they should properly be recognized both out of gratitude to God and in order to secure favorable auspices for the work in hand, I held that they should be reverently proclaimed, as they are, at the outset" (550). "I began by offering my most fervent thanks to almighty God. I would show that this proem, in which I offer so many convincing proofs that, although by no means exempt from the disasters common to humanity, I and my interests are nevertheless under the protection of God" (557). "I have been aided and enriched by the favor and assistance of God. Anything greater or more glorious than this I neither can, nor wish to, claim" (558).

another (Heavenly Muse, holy Light, Urania, Celestial Patroness, Spirit), and all of them set forth, from Milton's open heart, his sense of his relation with God. It is painful to have to limit these glorious passages to the personal testimony describing his sense of God.

The invocation to the First Book of *Paradise Lost* includes a general prayer for help, offering an "upright heart and pure" as a temple for God to dwell in and thus make possible the composition of the poem:

> And chiefly Thou O Spirit, that dost prefer
> Before all Temples th' upright heart and pure,
> Instruct me, for Thou know'st; Thou from the first
> Wast present, and with mighty wings outspread
> Dove-like satst brooding on the vast Abyss
> And mad'st it pregnant: What in me is dark
> Illumine, what is low raise and support;
> That to the highth of this great Argument
> I may assert Eternal Providence,
> And justify the ways of God to men.

The invocation to the Third Book, to holy Light, is a special prayer, in view of his blindness, for an interior illumination that will transcend human sight:

> So much the rather thou Celestial Light
> Shine inward, and the mind through all her powers
> Irradiate, there plant eyes, all mist from thence
> Purge and disperse, that I may see and tell
> Of things invisible to mortal sight.

The invocations to both the Seventh and the Ninth Books set forth Milton's grateful sense that he has been given personal divine guidance in composing the poem. The invocation to the Seventh Book, to heavenly Urania, tells of his being "fall'n on evil days…In darkness, and with dangers compast round / And solitude," but that he is

# The Inner Life

> …yet not alone, while thou
> Visit'st my slumbers Nightly, or when Morn
> Purples the East: still govern thou my Song,
> *Urania*, and fit audience find, though few.

In the Ninth Book, the invocation seeks the continuance of the divine guidance which has been with him throughout the writing of the poem:

> If answerable style I can obtain
> Of my Celestial Patroness, who deigns
> Her nightly visitation unimplor'd,
> And dictates to me slumb'ring, or inspires
> Easy my unpremeditated Verse.

In the invocation to *Paradise Regained*, Milton appeals directly to the Spirit of God for continued inspiration, without which (he says) he would be incapable of writing;

> Thou Spirit who led'st this glorious Eremite
> Into the Desert, his Victorious Field
> Against the Spiritual Foe, and brought'st him thence
> By proof th'undoubted Son of God, inspire,
> As thou art wont, my prompted Song, else mute,
> And bear through height or depth of nature's bounds
> With prosperous wing full summ'd to tell of deeds
> Above Heroic, though in secret done.

A spirit of humble confidence pervades all of these invocations. They are the words of someone who seems to feel personally at ease in his relationship with God, knowing that his talents will be well used. As the anonymous biographer (Cyriack Skinner, I, too, think it was) put it, "Yet did he not reckon this talent but as entrusted with him; and therefore dedicated all his labors to the glory of God and some public good."

It was in some such way as this that Milton thought and felt about his relation to God. These thoughts and feelings had, I believe, a controlling influence over every aspect of his life.

# John Milton

## II

Next to Milton's sense of God, and directly related to it, the most dominant force in his life was his sense of mission to be a poet. Possession of unusual abilities, or talent, was the first prerequisite, of course. "These abilities," wrote Milton in *Reason of Church-Government*, "wheresoever they be found, are the inspired guift of God rarely bestow'd, but yet to some (though most abuse) in every Nation" (*Prose*, I, 816).

But there were many other qualifications, as Milton viewed the role of the poet. First, a long and rigorous training. The poet needed a vast amount of learning; in particular, a thorough knowledge of languages and an extensive acquaintance with earlier literature, especially that of classical antiquity. To this "industrious and select reading" must be added "steddy observation" and "insight into all seemly and generous arts and affaires" (*Prose*, I, 821). The learning needed was much the same as that appropriate for a scholar, though the poet would wish to avoid the pedantry of mindless citation of authorities or fruitless work on texts. The training of the poet would usually involve an early beginning and a long continuing. There was so much to know that there would be little time for diversion, and none for sloth.

Milton was fortunate in having, while he was still young, at least one close friend who could try to get him to keep a balance to his life. That was Charles Diodati, of course. When they were still both university students, Diodati felt free (and felt it desirable) to give Milton (in a letter, in Greek) some advice which makes clear Milton's usual habits in the view of a talented, respected peer:

> Why do you despise the gifts of nature? Why such inexcusable perseverance, bending over books and studies day and night? Live, laugh, enjoy your youth and the hours, and stop reading the serious, the light, and the indolent works of ancient wise men, wearing yourself out the while. I, who in all other things am your inferior, in this one thing, in know-

ing the proper limit of labor, both seem to myself, and am, your better. Farewell, and be merry. (*Prose*, I, 337)

Of course Milton was often merry and he didn't always use "inexcusable perseverance, bending over books and studies day and night." At least we know that he became a good musician in the house of a good musician, playing the organ and the bass viol; he became a skilled swordsman; and he developed a lifelong habit of being a walker. But still there was his sense of mission to be a poet.

"My father destined me in early childhood," wrote Milton in the *Second Defence*, "for the study of literature."[4] There is a Biblical ring to "destined me in early childhood," as it was thus that mighty heroes–Samson, for example–were prepared for mighty tasks.

The life of learning was one altogether congenial to Milton. When he returned to Cambridge after a vacation in London, he wrote (in the Sixth Prolusion) that, "I fully intended at last to bury myself in learning and to devote myself day and night to the charms of philosophy" (*Prose*, I, 266). Even earlier, in the course of his rustication from Cambridge, he had written in Elegy I (to Diodati, 1626), "Here my hours are free to be dedicated to the quiet Muses; and my books, which are my life, quite carry me away." In 1642 he could sum up his efforts by saying that "none hath by more studious ways endeavour'd, and with more unwearied spirit that none shall, that I dare almost averre of my self, as farre as life and free leasure will extend" (*Reason of Church-Government*, *Prose*, I, 820).

In portraying the childhood of Christ in *Paradise Regained*, Milton thought it appropriate that Christ, in order to fulfill his ob-

---

4. *Prose*, IV, 612. In *Reason of Church-Government*, Milton had made the point in a somewhat different way: "I must say therefore that after I had from my first yeeres by the ceaselesse diligence and care of my father, whom God recompence, bin exercis'd to the tongues, and some sciences, as my age would suffer, by sundry masters and teachers both at home and at the schools" (*Prose*, I, 808-09).

ligation, should spend his childhood not in play but in learning:

> When I was yet a child, no childish play
> To me was pleasing, all my mind was set
> Serious to learn and know, and thence to do
> What might be public good. (I, 201-04)

Milton twice described (in *An Apology Against a Pamphlet* and in the *Second Defence*) the general course of his own education through childhood and the years that followed. That education included his study of languages, of classical orators and historians, the elegiac poets, classical philosophy, the Greek and Latin classics in general, mathematics and music, and the Christian religion. And he gave, in *Of Education*, a very much more detailed account of what he thought a proper course of study should consist; this curriculum—staggeringly extensive, and with such hints as that the Italian tongue may be "easily learnt at any odde hour"—was doubtless built around his own reading, though it does not include all of the subjects we know he studied nor all of the authors we know he read.

For Milton, a high degree of learning must be achieved before writing can be attempted. Trial and error on the part of an unlearned person was not a way that Milton favored. He did not think well of composing "Theams, verses and Orations" as exercises, because they are "the acts of ripest judgement and the finall work of a head fill'd by long reading, and observing, with elegant maxims, and copious invention" (*Prose*, II, 372).

Milton had had various glimmerings that he was destined to be a poet. In Elegy V (1629), he describes the sense of his poetic powers returning with the spring; in a letter to Diodati in 1637 he secretly admits, with embarrassment, that he has been thinking of immortality from writing poetry, and in the "Epitaphium Damonis" he tells of the British themes that he hopes to work out in English verse. "Ad Patrem" (about 1634) gives his fullest early statement of his commitment to poetry, however. He sees himself as a poet, above all else, and the opportunity to become a poet is

# The Inner Life

the greatest gift that could come from a father, excepting only the gift of heaven.

Milton's sense of mission cannot be satisfied simply by being "a writer." The "cool element of prose" does not suffice, for in that, he said, "I have the use, as I may account it, but of my left hand." His mission is to be "a Poet soaring in the high region of his fancies with his garland and singing robes about him" (*Reason of Church-Government*, *Prose*, I, 808).

It is perhaps in part because of his sense of the importance of poetry that Milton was so given to writing invocations for his poems. The invocation is ceremonial, a signal that a high kind of activity is underway, as he gathers his singing robes about him. Usually the invocations are quite personal; but the language about himself and about his role is relatively plain and straightforward, and the richness of tropes and of accumulative detail tends to cluster around the figure invoked rather than around the poet. The four great invocations in *Paradise Lost* and the one in *Paradise Regained* are enough to make him the master of the type in English, but we should not overlook the fact that a good many of the early poems also include invocations, sometimes a little hidden from view.[5]

Being a poet is a high mission. In Milton's view, it was undoubtedly the highest mission that a man could have. The Poet is a Maker in the human dimension, as God is the Maker (or true Creator) in the divine dimension, as Satan is the non-maker (or non-creator) in the infernal dimension.[6] Milton approached his

---

5. "At a Vacation Exercise," to his native language and his muse; "On the Morning of Christ's Nativity," to the Heav'nly Muse; "L'Allegro," to Mirth; "Il Penseroso," to Melancholy; "Upon the Circumcision," to the flaming Powers and winged warriors; "At a Solemn Music," to the blest pair of Sirens; "Ad Patrem," to his muse; "Lycidas," to the Muses; "Ad Salsillum," to his halting muse; and "Epitaphium Damonis," to the nymphs of Himera.

6. Satan is the Destroyer, as opposed to the Maker, and hence the non-Poet as well. He says:

mission with reverence about his vocation, with uncertainty about his present qualifications, but with confidence about his future success.

## III

For Milton, one further sense was inextricably bound up with his sense of God and with his sense of mission as a poet. That was his sense of virtue. This sense was actually an ideal of human behavior which would result, he thought, in a condition of life pleasing to God. Milton adopted an ideal of virtue which had been highly valued among writers of the Italian Renaissance, but he arrived at it in a peculiarly personal and literary way.

In the course of describing the program of his studies, he told of his delight in reading "the smooth Elegiack Poets" for recreation and in imitating them, but that at last he came to deplore them because their subjects were unworthy. From them he turned to Dante and Petrarch, whom he admired for their sublime and pure thoughts.

> And long it was not after [he continued], when I was confirm'd in this opinion, that he who would not be frustrate of his hope to write well hereafter in laudable things, ought him selfe to be a true Poem, that is, a composition, and patterne of the best and honourablest things; not presuming to sing high praises of heroick men, or famous Cities, unlesse he have in himselfe the experience and the practice of all that which is praise-worthy. (*An Apology Against a Pamphlet, Prose*, I, 890)

The poet's need for virtue—of which this is the classic expression—was deeply engrained in Milton's thinking. He repeated the

---

Nor hope to be myself less miserable
By what I seek, but others to make such
As I, though thereby worse to me redound:
For only in destroying I find ease
To my relentless thoughts. (*PL*, IX, 126-30)

14

idea several more times,[7] and he dilated on the moral responsibility that fell to the lot of the poet. (For Milton, the role of the poet in part paralleled and in part included the role of the orator.) It is worth re-reading an extended statement of his concept of the role of the poet to have clearly in mind his connection between the poet and virtue. The poet is, he said,

> to imbreed and cherish in a great people the seeds of vertu, and publick civility, to allay the perturbations of the mind, and set the affections in right tune, to celebrate in glorious and lofty Hymns the throne and equipage of Gods Almightinesse, and what he works, and what he suffers to be wrought with high providence in his Church, to sing the victorious agonies of Martyrs and Saints, the deeds and triumphs of just and pious Nations doing valiantly through faith against the enemies of Christ, to deplore the general relapses of Kingdoms and States from justice and Gods true worship. Lastly, whatsoever in religion is holy and sublime, in vertu amiable, or grave, whatsoever hath passion or admiration in all the changes of that which is call'd fortune from without, or the wily suttleties and refluxes of mans thoughts from within, all these things with a solid and treatable smoothnesse to paint out and describe. Teaching over the whole book of sanctity and vertu through all the instances of example with such delight to those especially of soft and delicious temper who will not so much as look upon Truth herselfe, unlesse they see her elegantly drest, that

7. "They expresse nature best, who in their lives least wander from her safe leading, which may be call'd regenerate reason. So that how he should be truly eloquent who is not withall a good man, I see not" (*Apology Against a Pamphlet, Prose*, I, 874). In responding to a request from Henry De Brass (letter 32, 1657) for advice on writing, Milton said: "I think thus: he who would write worthily of worthy deeds ought to write with no less largeness of spirit and experience of the world than he who did them, so that he can comprehend and judge as an equal even the greatest, and, having comprehended, can narrate them gravely and clearly in plain and temperate language" (*Prose*, VII, 501). And see Elegy VI on the high requirements for behavior and character and reputation for the epic poet.

15

whereas the paths of honesty and good life appear now rugged and difficult, though they be indeed easy and pleasant, they would then appear to all men both easy and pleasant though they were rugged and difficult indeed. (*Reason of Church-Government, Prose*, I, 816-18)

So much and more, much more, did Milton think the task of the poet. His was the task of extending the sense of virtue to the world around him. Milton associated the virtues with God. "God himself is truth!" he wrote. "The more veracious a man is in teaching truth to men, the more like must he be to God and the more acceptable to him" (*Second Defence, Prose*, IV, 585).[8]

Milton had a circle of associations which included God–love–virtue–truth–knowledge–poetry–liberty. "The first and chiefest office of love, begins and ends in the soule, producing those happy twins of her divine generation knowledge and vertue" (*An Apology Against a Pamphlet, Prose*, I, 892). His blindness "merely deprives things of color and superficial appearance. What is true and essential in them is not lost to my intellectual vision" (*Second Defence, Prose*, IV, 589). "There is nothing in human society more pleasing to God, or more agreeable to reason, nothing in the state more just, nothing more expedient, than the rule of the man most fit to rule...the liberator of your country, the author of liberty..." (671-72). The defence of liberty, as Milton saw it, was one of the main preoccupations of his life, and liberty was a part of general virtue. "What among human endeavors," he wrote to Oldenburg in 1654, "can be nobler or more useful than the protection of liberty" (*Prose*, IV, 866). Liberty and religion, Milton asserted, "God hath inseparably knit together" (*Prose*, I, 923). In his final effort to stave off the

---

8. "For who knows not that Truth is strong next to the Almighty" (*Areopagitica, Prose*, II, 562-63). In the 1630s Milton copied into his Commonplace Book the following entry and quotation under the heading "Of Lying": "How far it is permitted. A good man is always accustomed to speak the truth, says Clement, 'except as a form of healing, as when a physician for the safety of those who are suffering will lie to the sick or speak a falsehood.' & c. Strom: Book 7 p[age] 730" (*Prose*, I, 384).

# The Inner Life

Restoration of Charles II, in *The Readie & Easie Way*, Milton summed up his sense of freedom as a virtue: "The whole freedom of man consists either in spiritual or civil libertie. As for spiritual, who can be at rest, who can enjoy any thing in this world with contentment, who hath not libertie to serve God and to save his own soul, according to the best light which God hath planted in him to that purpose...?... The other part of our freedom consists in the civil rights and advancements of every person according to his merit..." (*Prose*, VII, 379, 383). The anonymous biographer was quite right, though he used language that seems quaint to our ears, when he called Milton "a constant champion for the liberty of opining."

## IV

One way of understanding Milton's sense of the self is to review, as I have tried to do, his sense of his relation to God as the great figure of authority in his life, his sense of his role of the poet as the great mission of his life, and his sense of virtue as the all-encompassing standard of human behavior.

Even from this most summary account, certain defining lines are clear. His bond with God was an understandable source of unwavering support and reassurance for him. His view of himself as a poet gave deep and continuing purpose to his life. His sense of virtue controlled his own behavior and his judgment of the behavior of other people.

Sonnet XIX ("When I consider how my light is spent") is built on, sums up, and clarifies a good many of these basic themes of Milton's sense of the self. Although sometimes called Milton's best-known sonnet, I think it is not the best understood one. I would like to offer a commentary on this poem as a kind of resting place for the discussion up to this point.

### Sonnet XIX

When I consider how my light is spent,
Ere half my days, in this dark world and wide,
And that one Talent which is death to hide,

# John Milton

Lodg'd with me useless, though my Soul more bent
To serve therewith my Maker, and present
My true account, lest he returning chide;
"Doth God exact day-labor, light denied,"
I fondly ask; But patience to prevent
That murmur, soon replies, "God doth not need
Either man's work or his own gifts; who best
Bear his mild yoke, they serve him best; his State
Is Kingly. Thousands at his bidding speed
And post o'er Land and Ocean without rest:
They also serve who only stand and wait."

This sonnet is an expression of Milton's sense of himself at a time that turned out to be the very middle of his career. He had recently become totally blind; the poem was written sometime between 1651 and 1655, when he was about forty-two to forty-six.[9] Many poems and many prose works were behind him, of high merit as we think, to him not quite satisfying. His question was: What lies ahead for the blind man? Still in front of him, as he could not know, were more prose works and—the climax of his artistic life—truly major poems, perhaps the best we have in English, enough (one would think) to satisfy the most demanding standard of value.

The sonnet. In a flash, he reviews his use of his sight when he had it. Now blind, he can't make his talent serve God, though he wants to, more than ever. Will God condemn him when the time of reckoning comes? Or will God require the blind man to perform work of which he may be incapable? A foolish question, self-serving, foreshadowing a grumble. As if God needed his work! God is beyond the need of man's work or gifts. Man's best service is to accept God's will. Thousands serve the omnipotent King by action; others can serve him by waiting for his direction.

9. Most of the commentary on the poem concerns the dating of it, the relation of the date to the beginning of Milton's blindness, the meaning of "ere half my days," and the like. Fortunately, neither a review nor a resolution of these problems—which so far seem unsolvable—is necessary for the purposes of this discussion.

# The Inner Life

The principal inadequacy of this or any other prose paraphrase—however desirable it is as a place to begin—is its failure to convey any sense of the richness or texture of the poem. That richness, which is conveyed only by the poem itself, comes principally from the reverberations of the running allusions to two parables.

Through the first six lines, it is the Parable of the Talents, in the Matthew version (25: 14-30). The servant who was given one talent reported to his Lord, "I was afraid, and went and hid my talent in the earth"; when he gave it back to his lord, he was judged "wicked and slothful" and, as an "unprofitable servant," was cast "into outer darkness" where "there shall be weeping and gnashing of teeth." Milton's fear is that, since his talent is lodged with him useless, he may likewise be judged a "wicked and slothful" servant and be cast "into outer darkness."[10]

From the whole drift of the discussion that has gone before in this chapter, it seems to me plain that the "one Talent" of the sonnet refers to Milton's ability as a poet: that is the native, God-entrusted ability that matters to him above all else.[11] As to why he gives himself one talent, rather than two or five, it would be a

10. I found the Parable of the Talents more vividly understandable after seeing an actual talent—massive, heavy, impressive. The one I first saw, in the museum at Heraklion, was a copper ingot about 15″ by 18″ by 2″, said to weigh some 66 pounds. Although they were of somewhat different weights (and sizes) in different areas and different periods of the ancient world, all were relatively heavy, all plausible as an object to bury in the ground. (It is interesting to notice that the New English Bible renders the term as "bag of gold.")

I found the parable clearer upon realizing that the literal sense of the term talent was still strong in Milton's time, that the figurative sense of talent as mental endowment or natural ability was derived from the Parable of the Talents and carried the association of divinely entrusted (many OED entries), and that our normal current sense of special ability or aptitude (without divine endowment implied) was new in Milton's time (only four OED entries before 1650, the first in 1600).

11. Most commentators think otherwise. Parker insists that it is the "capacity for composing a truly great poem" (p. 470). I think that Parker's reading of the sonnet as "a flat rejection of the whole point of the parable of the talents" (p. 471) is absurd.

mistake to make too much of the idea that Milton is practising a little humility in his choice, though humility is a welcome side effect, like sitting at the foot of the table till you are urged to move up; what is principally important is that it was the situation of the one-talent man (not the two or the five) in the parable that aroused his own anxiety about himself, and he therefore had to apply the whole situation to himself; finally, he had long thought of himself (the parable aside) as a person divinely endowed with one very special ability, not two or five. He longs to give a "true account" of that ability, both because his soul (that "divine particle of Gods breathing") wishes to have an ever closer bond with God and because he does not want to suffer the consequences that came to the one-talent man in the parable.

Milton seems to have had a special interest in the Parable of the Talents, as he alludes to it several times. In the first draft of a letter (of about 1633) Milton answers an unknown friend, who had apparently urged him to give over his search for knowledge and instead seek preferment in some good post, by saying, "but what delight or what peculiar conceit, may you in charitie thinke, could hold out against the long knowledge of a contrarie command from above, & the terrible seasure of him that hid his talent" (*Works*, XII, 321). In the second draft of the letter, the threat of the parable still hangs over him, to be sure that his love of learning accords with "due & tymely obedience to that command in the gospell set out by the terrible seasing of him that hid the talent" (*Works*, XII, 324).

It is the plight of the one-talent man that worries Milton. He will not listen to the blandishments of someone who wants him to deviate from what he considers God's commandment for him to use his talent. In *Reason of Church-Government*, Milton alludes again to God's final reckoning in the parable of the use of talents when he says that "God even to a strictnesse requires the improvment of these his entrusted gifts...which God hath sent him into this world to trade with" (*Prose*, I, 801).

It is worth observing that the side note in the Geneva Bible (1560 edition) to the chapter heading for the Parable of the Talents says that by the similitude of the talents Jesus teaches us to be diligent. Milton hardly needed this urging, nor the picture of the "terrible seasure" of the "wicked and slothful servant," but he apparently felt that he did. Somehow, getting up early and working late didn't give him confidence that he would escape the reckoning without condemnation. Milton was tough on himself, and his God (like Milton) has very high standards and is not inclined to let down the bars.[12]

The first six lines of the sonnet use the Parable of the Talents to set a question and expose a deep fear. The limits of allusion within the parable would, if pursued, allow only an answer of failure and death. So Milton deftly shifts the base of allusion at line 7 (and for the remainder of the sonnet) to the Parable of the Vineyard (Matthew 20: 1-16). The "day-labor" of line 7 and

12. Much of the contemporary religious literature on like subjects was certainly in tune with that view. This exhortation on the parable of the rich man who called his steward to account is, I think, a fair example: "Tremble and quake (O sinner) at the cogitation of these things. Repent, reuert, and turne vnto the Lord. For what art thou to stand in the presence of this Iudge; being fraile, vaine, weake, naked miserable, filthy, and horrible?" (Robert Bagnall, *The Stewards Last Account: Delivered in Five Sermons vpon the sixteenth chapter of the Gospell by Saint Luke, the first and second Verses*, London, 1622, p. 69).

Or this commentary on Luke xii. 48: *"For to whom much is giuen of him much shall be required.* This in the first place, not to reioice though in miraculous effects of graces bestowed vpon him, but rather in that his name is written in the booke of life, in whose golden lines none are enfraunchised but such as in pouerty of spirit haue serued an apprentiship to humility. Thus may the brother of lowest degree, so he will not be wilfully proud, nor stretch his desires beyond *the measure God hath distributed to him"* (Thomas Jackson, *Iustifying Faith, or The Faith by which the Just do liue*, London, 1615, p. 304).

A meditation (of seven pages) on the Parable of the Talents is included in Luis de la Puente, *Meditations upon the Mysteries of our Holie Faith* (St. Omers, 1619), I, 777-84. This meditation (by a Jesuit, translated into English for the benefit of "all deceaued Protestants") glorifies diligence and industry while condemning sloth as the sin which caused the one-talent man to be cast "into the exterior darknes of hell."

Compendia of moral philosophy included quotations to a similar effect, attributed to likely and unlikely sources. These, for example, from William Baldwin's *Treatise of Morall Phylosophie, contaynyng the sayinges of the wyse:* "God wyl rewarde euery man according to hys woorkes. Hermes"; "No man may escape the iust iudgement of God. Aristotle" (London, 1547, p. I 3ʳ).

those "who only stand and wait" of the last line enclose the allusion to laborers who stand in the marketplace waiting for the lord of the vineyard to give them employment, whether early in the morning, or at the third, sixth, ninth, or eleventh hour of the day, while those already chosen are serving in the vineyard.

Milton apparently associated in his own mind these two parables (which are both Parables of the Kingdom) on the theme "The kingdom of heaven is like unto...." In the letter to an unknown friend to which I have already referred, Milton joins the two parables and assumes that they are both applicable as ways of responding to the charge that he had too much given himself up to studious retirement. After asserting his obligation to use the talent given him, by referring to the need for "due & tymely obedience to that command in the gospell set out by the terrible seasing of him that hid the talent," he goes on and, in the very next sentence, says that "this very consideration of that great commandment does not presse forward as soone as may be to undergoe but keeps off with a sacred reverence, & religious advisement how best to undergoe not taking thought of beeing late so it give advantage to be more fit, for those that were latest lost nothing when the maister of the vinyard came to give each one his hire."[13]

The last eight lines of the sonnet give a reassuring answer to the question, and they quiet the deep fear. At the same time, the point of view shifts from that of the speaker–Milton, man–in the first six lines toward that of God in the last eight lines. Without

13. Milton was aware that his shift from one parable to another in this letter made it possible for him to support both sides of the argument at once. His letter continues: "Heere I am come to a streame head [the Parable of the Vineyard] copious enough to disburden it selfe like Nilus at seven mouthes into an ocean, but then I should also run into a reciprocall contradiction of ebbing & flowing at once & doe that which I excuse my selfe for not doing preach & not preach. yet that you may see that I am something suspicious of my selfe, & doe take notice of a certaine belatednesse in me I am the bolder to send you some of my nightward thoughts" (*Works*, XII, 324-25). And he writes out in his letter the sonnet "How soon hath Time" as proof of his activity. (I quote passages from this letter from *Works* rather than *Prose*, as only the former gives both drafts of the letter.)

# The Inner Life

minimizing the importance of service through action ("Thousands at his bidding speed / And post o'er Land and Ocean without rest"), the sonnet extends the idea of service to include inaction. The great supervening truth is acquiescence to the will of God ("who best / Bear his mild yoke, they serve him best," whatever state or condition is given them). The sonnet began in uncertainty, it moved through disquiet and fear, it ends with a sense of peace and calm. "They also serve who only stand and wait."

# Chapter II
## The Sense of the Self

### INNER DRIVES

IDEALS BECOME OPERATIVE through desire. It is the desire to fulfill ideals of human behavior that gives them concrete meaning. Milton's central ideals—his informing values—were (as I see them) his sense of relationship with God, of his mission as a poet, and of the centrality of virtue. I have tried to set forth the basis for that proposition in the preceding chapter. What does that proposition mean, so far as our understanding of Milton is concerned?

Throughout Milton's writings about himself, one is conscious of his awareness that he is someone quite special—particularly chosen, unusually talented, especially perceptive—and of his sense of responsibility for living up to the rare gifts that had been bestowed on him. Milton was the sort of person we are inclined to typify as an idealist. He was one of that small group of persons who have an important element of altruism in their makeup, who have an awareness of their own value systems, who try to live in accordance with that value system, and who may sometimes ignore (or be irritated by) real difficulties that keep them from fulfilling their wishes, even though those difficulties are beyond their effective control.[1]

A key problem that Milton—along with many others—faced was learning how to deal with his sense of obligation while fulfill-

1. Milton's idealism is one of the principal themes of Parker's biography. See for example, vol. I, pp. 23, 28, 109-10, 226-30, 240, 276, 347, 530, 590. While I am not sure that I know how broad the term "idealism" is in Parker's use, I believe that his views generally support the interpretation that I offer.

ing the responsibilities that seemed to devolve on him. In this chapter, I would like to discuss four topics which relate to his efforts and to his deep attitude toward this problem. First, what Milton did to try to meet what he conceived to be his obligation. Second, his response when that line of action was not entirely successful. Third, the nature and object of the drive in him that we call ambition. And fourth, the revelations about his desires as they come out in indirect ways.

I

Milton's principal tactic in meeting his sense of high responsibility was a very simple one. It is the same tactic that is employed by many people who try to live up to–and feel comfortable with–a very high standard that they have set for themselves, or that has been imposed on them. That tactic is hard work–hard work beyond the normal level of effort.

We remember Milton's account, in the *Second Defence* (1654), of his commitment to literature. "My father destined me in early childhood for the study of literature." But the sentence continues: "for which I had so keen an appetite that from my twelfth year scarcely ever did I leave my studies for my bed before the hour of midnight" (*Prose*, IV, 612). It is a sentence that is doubtless a literal account of Milton's style of life, at least during this period of more than thirty years–"scarcely ever did I leave my studies for my bed before the hour of midnight."

Milton's style of life impressed his early biographers, who described (with something like awe) his habit of hard work carried through long hours. Here are three samples which are moderately independent of one another.

John Aubrey: "From his bro. Chr. Milton:–When he went to school, when he was very young, he studied very hard, and sat up very late; commonly till 12 or one o'clock at night, and his father ordered the maid to sit up for him, and in those years (10) composed many copies of verses, which might well become a riper age. And was a very hard student in the university, and performed all his exercises there with very good applause" (Hughes, p. 1023).

Edward Phillips: Before Milton went to Cambridge, he had "insuperable industry: for he generally sat up half the night, as well in voluntary improvements of his own choice, as the exact perfecting of his school exercises. So that at the age of 15 he was full ripe for academic learning, and accordingly was sent to the University of Cambridge" (Hughes, p. 1027).

The anonymous biographer: "through the pregnancy of his parts and his indefatigable industry (sitting up constantly at his study till midnight), he profited exceedingly" (Hughes, p. 1038).

It was late to bed, and it was also early to rise. Milton was very particular in describing (in *Apology*) his hours for getting up, as if he took pride in these habits as a form of moral superiority: "up, and stirring, in winter often ere the sound of any bell awake men to labour, or to devotion; in Summer as oft with the Bird that first rouses, or not much tardier, to read good Authors, or cause them to be read, till the attention bee weary, or memory have his full fraught" (*Prose*, I, 885).

Hard work was to be a lifelong habit with him. Milton thought of himself as a single-minded person strongly driven to accomplish his objectives. Concentration and orderliness were central qualities of his makeup. To Charles Diodati he wrote openly and revealingly (in Letter 7, 1637) that "your habit of studying permits you to pause frequently, visit friends, write much, and sometimes make a journey. But my temperament allows no delay, no rest, no anxiety–or at least thought–about scarcely anything to distract me, until I attain my object and complete some great period, as it were, of my studies" (*Prose*, I, 323). The drive Milton felt was directed at reaching a goal. The goal changed for him from time to time, but the drive remained constant.

Writing, like studying, was for Milton an arduous task. He gives a vignette of the writer at work in *Areopagitica:* "When a man writes to the world, he summons up all his reason and deliberation to assist him; he searches, meditats, is industrious, and likely consults and conferrs with his judicious friends; after all which done he takes himself to be inform'd in what he writes, as well as any that writ before him." This is "the most consummat act of his fidelity and ripenesse," the fruit of "all his considerat diligence, all his midnight watchings, and expence of *Palladian* oyl" (*Prose*, II, 532). (Here is that midnight work again!) The inference is that such special industry and diligence can or should or will result in writings that the world would take note of.

Others could indulge in diversions. But Milton could never do so easily, because of his commitment to work. "An idle liesure has never pleased me." So he wrote, in 1654, to Henry Oldenburg (*Prose*, IV, 866). Indeed not. Another term for idle ease in Milton's vocabulary is sloth, against which he was unusually vehement in his condemnation.

In his earliest extant composition, the "Theme on Early Rising" (presumed to have been written at the age of fifteen or sixteen while at St. Paul's School), his negative arguments are mostly against sloth. "Up then, up, you sluggard, and let not soft sheets keep you forever.... A good ruler should not grow fat in endless slumber and live a life of leisure and empty ease.... What can be more shameful than to snore late into the day and to devote the greatest part of your life to a sort of death?" (*Prose*, I, 1037-39). These are stock details, but they are the details that the young Milton chose as persuasive arguments. And they are the same kind of details that recur in his other writings, such as "Carmina Elegiaca" and "Ignavus satrapam dedecet." We remember that Belial's plea for peace is put down with special sharpness on the grounds that what he was counselling was really "ignoble ease, and peaceful sloth" (*PL*, II, 227).

Milton's entry under "Sloth" in his Commonplace Book (thought to have been written in 1635-38?) gives a summary of some lines from Dante. "The punishment, in the infernal regions, of the slothful who have done nothing in this life well, nor anything which is notably evil, is described by Dante of Florence; they are agitated in vain by perpetual disquiet and by a certain gad-fly. Dante Inferno. cant: 3" (*Prose*, I, 384). Milton's

# The Inner Life

apparent acceptance of the idea of sloth as lack of noteworthy achievement is compatible with his feeling for the importance of hard work as the road to important objectives.

Let me quote again the lines spoken by Christ about his habit, like Milton's, of avoiding diversion and concentrating on work, in the thought that it will have greater meaning in this context:

> When I was yet a child, no childish play
> To me was pleasing, all my mind was set
> Serious to learn and know, and thence to do
> What might be public good. (*PR*, I, 201-04)

As Milton set a high and single-minded standard for the endeavor of Christ, so he did for his own work. While still a student, he lays out almost impossibly high standards for himself. "I have learnt from the writings and sayings of wise men," he wrote in the Seventh Prolusion, "that nothing common or mediocre can be tolerated in an orator any more than in a poet, and that he who would be an orator [or a poet] in reality as well as by repute must first acquire a thorough knowledge of all the arts and sciences to form a complete background to his own calling" (*Prose*, I, 288-89).

*Complete.* That is the word. Whatever it is must be *complete* before you can feel right about moving on. Another key is *perfection.* It was nothing less than *perfection* that was his final goal. "Last of all," he wrote in the *Apology,* "not in time, but as perfection is last..." (*Prose*, I, 892). It is no wonder that Milton felt driven to work long and late.

## II

The tactic of hard work contributed, in Milton, to the making of a learned man. He could have become a first-class scholar or, today, a star in the academic firmament of research professors. But, unfortunately for him, hard work did not bring him the satisfaction of feeling that he had fulfilled the talent that he thought his chiefest possession.

29

# John Milton

He took the undertaking of poetry as his central public mission. And yet, for many years into maturity—perhaps even for his entire career—he still did not feel quite ready to embark, with full confidence, on his chosen career as a poet.

His sonnet on Shakespeare, written when he was about twenty-two, expresses the yearning of the unfulfilled poet for those "easy numbers" of Shakespeare, as opposed to the "shame of slow-endeavoring art"—which presumably included himself. And yet the yearning can't be satisfied by extra work: try very hard to attain the ideal of Shakespeare and the effort "dost make us Marble with too much conceiving."

A year or two later, Milton wrote one of his greatest and most touching sonnets, about himself as an unfulfilled poet. It is a lamentation, really, but without self-pity, about his lack of satisfaction from his efforts to become a poet, about his aging through the inexorable passage of time, and about his need to reconcile himself to these realities.

Sonnet VII

How Soon Hath Time

How soon hath Time, the subtle thief of youth,
    Stol'n on his wing my three and twentieth year!
    My hasting days fly on with full career,
    But my late spring no bud or blossom show'th.
Perhaps my semblance might deceive the truth,
    That I to manhood am arriv'd so near,
    And inward ripeness doth much less appear,
    That some more timely-happy spirits endu'th.
Yet be it less or more, or soon or slow,
    It shall be still in strictest measure ev'n
    To that same lot, however mean or high,
Toward which Time leads me, and the will of Heav'n;
    All is, if I have grace to use it so,
    As ever in my great task-Master's eye.

The poem presents us, in a conventionally public way, with Milton's private image of himself. He sees himself as lacking in achievement appropriate to his age, and he views himself as a late bloomer. He confesses that he thinks he looks younger than the twenty-three (or more) that he actually is; he is confident that he does have a measure of inner maturity, even though it is not so evident as it is for those who look their age. How can he reconcile himself to the fact that he has not done more in the years he has had? He gives a plain and simple answer: keep the faith, resign himself to the working out of God's will whenever and however that may come to pass, and use his talents faithfully in the meantime.

I do not know whether that answer did or did not satisfy Milton when he wrote it. He undoubtedly believed in it as a "right" answer, which it certainly is, within his Christian tradition. But I doubt that it really gave him inner peace.

At least, that answer did not settle the question for him. The same kind of question keeps recurring in his writings over the next decade or two, and he has a hard time dealing with it.

My feeling is that the concept of time did not worry Milton abstractly or philosophically, but it did personally. He was himself getting older in time without as much to show for his years as he thought appropriate, given his talent and his hard work. How can he deal with the pressing reality of this lack?

A year or two after Sonnet VII, he composed "On Time," which is a further commentary on that "subtle thief of youth" and almost a gloss on the sonnet. In the sonnet, time is a human measure of the adequacy of achievements and the appropriateness of appearances, with the resolution to accept (as the will of heaven) where you find yourself according to that measure.

"On Time" tackles the problem in a different way. It denigrates the worthiness of Time as a proper measure and sets up Eternity (or timelessness) as the true measure. The poem is achieved by the association of value words with the two concepts. With Time, the value words are: envious, lazy leaden-stepping, heavy Plummet, glut, womb devours, false and vain, mortal dross, loss, bad entomb'd, greedy self consum'd. With Eternity, the value words are: bliss, kiss, Joy, sincerely good, perfectly divine, Truth, Peace, Love, supreme Throne, happy-making, heav'nly-guided, for ever, Triumphing. The poem has its own truth, but it is also a way for Milton to reconcile his personal sense of belatedness about his achievements. There will be plenty of time in the future to do all that can and should be done.[2]

For a person who values current achievement, however, the present is the measure. For Milton, the present was troublesome. In a remarkably open and candid letter of about 1633 to a friend (apparently Thomas Young, his old teacher at St. Paul's School) Milton thanks him for his admonition to work hard and he freely acknowledges the unsatisfactory state of his present life: "I call my life as yet obscure, & unserviceable to mankind." He says that Young is wrong, however, in attributing his failure to "too much love of Learning" or that "I have given up my selfe to dreame away my Yeares in the armes of studious retirement." The drive to have a house and family and "credible employment" usually moves men at about his age, he admits; but he has the equally potent drive of the true scholar in "a desire of honour & repute, & immortall fame," and in the knowledge of the high value of his pursuit. He admits his slowness but argues in favor of "not taking thought of beeing late so it give advantage to be more fit, for those that were latest lost nothing when the maister of the vinyard came to give each one his hire."

After all of this reasoning, however, Milton recognizes that he may be simply rationalizing for his own benefit. "Yet you may see," he concludes, "that I am something suspicio[us] of my selfe, & doe take notice of a certaine belatednesse in me." That is the heart of the matter. There was, for Milton, "a certaine belatednesse" in himself. He did not like it, and he apparently didn't

---

2. Milton associated Time and Death in *Paradise Lost*. Sin says to Death: "whatever thing / The Scythe of Time mows down, devour unspar'd" (X, 605-06). Adam's last speech, to Michael, touches the relation of time and eternity:

> this transient World, the Race of time,
> Till time stand fixt: beyond is all abyss,
> Eternity, whose end no eye can reach. (XII, 554-56)

know what else to do about it except to drive ahead and work hard (*Prose*, I, 319-20).

As an earnest of his efforts, Milton enclosed one of his poems for Thomas Young to read. What did Milton think of as an appropriate enclosure? He sent the sonnet beginning "How soon hath Time, the subtle thief of youth."

That was about 1633. Some four years later, when Milton was around twenty-nine, he lamented the necessity for having to compose a poem before the time when he felt ready to write. The occasion was the death of Edward King, and the poem was "Lycidas."

The familiar opening lines of that poem are, within the governing conventions, an intimate picture of Milton's feelings about writing and about himself. Indeed they have some of the essence of Milton in them:

> Yet once more, O ye Laurels, and once more
> Ye Myrtles brown, with Ivy never sere,
> I come to pluck your Berries harsh and crude,
> And with forc'd fingers rude,
> Shatter your leaves before the mellowing year.
> Bitter constraint, and sad occasion dear,
> Compels me to disturb your season due.

He succeeded in overcoming his scruples and in giving us the poem, and we rejoice that he did so. But for him the time was not yet ripe.

In 1642, at the age of thirty-four, he still felt that his studies were incomplete and that he was not yet ready to write, even though he had worked hard. Again he had to overcome his scruples. "I should not write thus out of mine own season," he says in *Reason of Church-Government*, "when I have neither yet compleated to my minde the full circle of my private studies, although I complain not of any insufficiency to the matter in hand" (*Prose*, I, 807).

At the same time, he felt guarded confidence in the likelihood of future achievements. He tells us, in words that have the ring of

# John Milton

immortality about them, that his teachers had told him that his "stile by certain vital signes it had, was likely to live." After being praised in Italy for his writing, "I began thus farre to assent both to them and divers of my friends here at home, and not lesse to an inward prompting which now grew daily upon me, that by labour and intent study (which I take to be my portion in this life) joyn'd with the strong propensity of nature, I might perhaps leave something so written to aftertimes, as they should not willingly let it die" (*Prose*, I, 809-10).

That is for the future. His feeling of confidence about that future is cautious, governed by "might" and "perhaps," but still real. For the earnest present, it must continue to be "labour and intent study (which I take to be my portion in this life)." He seems to have reached a delicate balance of peace within himself about fulfilling his obligations.

He can offer, freely and openly, a solemn pledge about what he will promise to do for his part in trying to live up to his talents:

> Neither doe I think it shame to covnant with any knowing reader, that for some few yeers yet I may go on trust with him toward the payment of what I am now indebted, as being a work not to be rays'd from the heat of youth, or the vapours of wine, like that which flows at wast from the pen of some vulgar Amorist, or the trencher fury of a riming parasite, nor to be obtain'd by the invocation of Dame Memory and her Siren daughters, but by devout prayer to that eternall Spirit who can enrich with all utterance and knowledge, and sends out his Seraphim with the hallow'd fire of his Altar to touch and purify the lips of whom he pleases: to this must be added industrious and select reading, steddy observation, insight into all seemly and generous arts and affaires, till which in some measure be compast, at mine own peril and cost I refuse not to sustain this expectation from as many as are not loath to hazard so much credulity upon the best pledges that I can give them. (*Prose*, I, 820-21)

34

# The Inner Life

This covenant is presented with the finality of a legal indenture and with the solemnity of a religious ritual. He carried out his covenant with strict exactness. His later words on this subject—as in the invocations to *Paradise Lost*, almost twenty-five years later—echo the spirit of the commitment made here. So did Milton pledge that he would fulfill his sense of self. And so he did.

Even so, he continued to feel a bit of uneasiness about his lack of current achievement. Sometimes he bent chronology a little, presumably so that his belatedness would seem less marked.

In the *Second Defence*, Milton said (in response to a silly attack on his appearance) that "although I am past forty, there is scarcely anyone to whom I do not seem younger by about ten years" (*Prose*, IV, 583). In the winter and spring of 1654, when he was writing that pamphlet, he was indeed "past forty"; he was in fact a little over forty-five. He has moved the feast back by five years. There is, moreover, a touch of vanity—or abandonment of real-ity—in a forty-five year old man exulting in the notion that others thought he looked about thirty or so.

Milton's dating of his own poems raises a good many ques-tions, always as to whether he was really as young as he claimed when he wrote the poem. There is, about the dating, a suggestion that Milton wanted to appear as young as possible. We might think: In order to minimize, in his own mind, his sense of belat-edness? In order to increase his sense of accomplishment? It is certain in two instances that he was older, by a couple of years, than he claimed to be. About the others, the scholarly world is still vibrating in a state of uncertainty as to whether he was as young as he claimed to be, or whether he was not.[3]

---

3. Milton's dating of his own poems is one of the stickiest topics I know about. It has engaged the attention of some of our leading scholars, and there has been extensive—many would say excessive—writing on the subject. I expect that dating problems have now outstripped the two-handed engine in contribu-tions to "the Milton literature."

The two instances in which Milton was plainly wrong are: 1) "On the Death of the Vice-Chancellor," which Milton dated "Anno Aetatis 16." But the Vice

# John Milton

## III

Milton wanted to live up to the high level of his talents. But he also had another clear drive. That was his ambition for fame as a poet.

Even as an undergraduate, he set a high value on fame. It is interesting to notice in the Seventh Prolusion the arguments he chose to use—following the classical tradition—in support of the topic that learning brings more blessings to men than ignorance does. He makes a special point of arguing that one of the rewards of study can be fame. That is, he says

> a pleasure with which none can compare—to be the oracle of many nations, to find one's home regarded as a kind of temple, to be a man whom kings and states invite to come to them, whom men from near and far flock to visit, while to others it is a matter for pride if they have but set eyes on him once. (*Prose*, I, 297)

What a wide-eyed expectation to be able to imagine, even if only as a manufactured support for a set argument! And one thinks of his later pleasure in receiving visits from foreigners who sought him out, and of the satisfaction in his repeated references to Queen Christina of Sweden for her favorable allusion to him.

Further in that same Seventh Prolusion, Milton enlists the prospect of Christian immortality as a further support of fame. His not-very-Christian argument is that you will still be able to enjoy the praise of your performance on earth after you have passed along to your reward:

---

Chancellor didn't die until October 21, 1626, when Milton was only six weeks short of being eighteen years old. 2) "On the Death of a Fair Infant Dying of a Cough," which Milton dated "Anno Aetatis 17." But the fair infant didn't die until January 1628, when Milton was already 19.

Parker gives a full resumé (pp. 784-87) of the facts and the scholarship about the ten poems that Milton dated with the "Anno Aetatis" formula. There is much more on dating the sonnets (and *Samson Agonistes*!), but they raise other problems.

Of the nine familiar letters before 1641 which were printed in 1674, Milton seems to have misdated two or three, again always earlier than the actual date.

to have no thought of glory when we do well is above all glory. The ancients could indeed derive no satisfaction from the empty praise of men, seeing that no joy or knowledge of it could reach them when they were dead and gone. But we may hope for an eternal life, which will never allow the memory of the good deeds we performed on earth to perish; in which, if we have done well here, we shall ourselves be present to hear our praise. (*Prose*, I, 302)

And to enjoy it, too, one supposes! Of course it is a little unfair to take youthful effusions altogether seriously. But in Milton's case, at least, they point in the direction that he continued to move.

In maturity, Milton kept lamenting his obscurity and expressing his desire for fame. In the letter of 1633 to Thomas Young (to which I have already referred) Milton speaks of the desire "to dissuade prolonged obscurity, a desire of honour & repute, & immortall fame seated in the brest of every true scholar w$^{ch}$ all make hast to by the readiest ways of publishing & divulging conceived merits" (*Prose*, I, 319-20).

In the "Epitaphium Damonis," when Milton tells (11. 161-78) of his plan to write an epic about Britain in English verse, he expresses reluctant willingness to give up international fame; if read in Britain, "I shall have ample reward and think my glory great—though I may be forever unknown and inglorious throughout all the outside world." This concession suggests vast self-confidence; it was made (we remember) by someone who had published only a few poems and who was virtually unknown.

In *Eikonoklastes*, Milton begins his Preface by saying that he isn't trying to get a name "by writing against a King." "I never was so thirsty after Fame," he goes on, "nor so destitute of other hopes and means, better and more certaine to attaine it." He continues, in a rather superior tone, that "no man ever gain'd much honour by writing against a King" (*Prose*, III, 337). From all of which we may infer that ways of gaining fame and honor were not far down on his priority list.

The classic passage about fame is, of course, in "Lycidas" and I

believe that our understanding of it can be enriched by discussing
it in this context:

> Alas! What boots it with uncessant care
> To tend the homely slighted Shepherd's trade,
> And strictly meditate the thankless Muse?
> Were it not better done as others use,
> To sport with *Amaryllis* in the shade,
> Or with the tangles of *Neaera's* hair?
> *Fame* is the spur that the clear spirit doth raise
> (That last infirmity of Noble mind)
> To scorn delights, and live laborious days;
> But the fair Guerdon when we hope to find,
> And think to burst out into sudden blaze,
> Comes the blind *Fury* with th'abhorred shears,
> And slits the thin-spun life. "But not the praise,"
> *Phoebus* repli'd, and touch'd my trembling ears;
> "*Fame* is no plant that grows on mortal soil,
> Nor in the glistering foil
> Set off to th'world, nor in broad rumor lies,
> But lives and spreads aloft by those pure eyes
> And perfect witness of all-judging *Jove*;
> As he pronounces lastly on each deed,
> Of so much fame in Heav'n expect thy meed." (64-84)

In this dense passage, Milton is up to his regular trick of seeming to solve problems by asking questions. The first six lines are
all questions, all loaded questions, about the value of spending
your life in the hard and thankless task of writing poetry instead
of in sensual delights. The questions, we notice, are all loaded the
wrong way. Milton is superb at giving appeal to a choice that he
doesn't himself really believe in—though doubtless a little of his
heart is always in the false choice.

This tactic of Milton's is what has made him seem to be of the
Devil's party without knowing it, and it is a tactic that deserves a
brief digression. Blake's reflection was (I think) mistaken as a literal comment but true as a general perception about Milton's

entire sensibility. Blake was flowing with the surface action of *Paradise Lost* but not in touch with the deeper currents. Milton gives some of his very best poetry to the villains (Satan and Comus, for example), and the villains almost always have more lavish poetry than do the heroes. Many readers have felt that Milton's heart was therefore with the villains, and that they were his heroes. This is, I believe, not true. It is not just that vice is more attractive and appealing than virtue, to readers and writers alike, as Fielding so wonderfully set it forth in *Tom Jones*. In Milton, the villain is always involved in a combat with a hero over an important issue, and the villain has intrinsically a weak position to work from. Milton the rhetorician steps up and goes to special pains to balance the combat. He strengthens the effect of what the villain has to say by maximizing the use of the flowers of eloquence in setting forth his argument. Some readers fall for the rhetoric. But Milton never lets a villain get away with anything; the villain is always checked, and answered, and demolished.

To return to "Lycidas," and the passage on fame. In this case, part of Milton's heart was in the false choice because he doubtless did get tired of working over poems, and he was sorry not to get much acclaim, and he probably did have some longing for the sportive play that Diodati commended. These feelings, secondary to begin with, are suppressed by his sense of obligation to fulfill his talent.

Then in line 7 comes a ringing affirmation: "*Fame* is the spur that the clear spirit doth raise." This memorable line sounds like—and is often taken as—the answer to all of those personal questions that bedeviled Milton's sense of ideal self-confidence, and the self-confidence of every person who gives up attractive or appealing alternatives for the sake of the concentrated effort thought necessary for achieving goals. Working instead of playing golf on Saturday, writing books in the evening instead of going to the theater, convincing yourself that your work is really your recreation and that vacations are therefore unnecessary. Undoubtedly Milton, like everybody else, occasionally had nagging doubts about his sense of values, that maybe he had made a mistake to give up so much for what at the moment seemed so little. But not for long: his sense of values was deeply fixed in him.

"*Fame* is the spur." In *Paradise Regained*, Milton has Satan use the same argument to Christ about fame as the spur:

> The fame and glory, glory the reward
> That sole excites in high attempts. (III, 25-26)

That might be the answer, if you could find a way to live with it by making fame the highest value.

But at best it is only a limited answer. As Milton is at pains to point out in the very next line of "Lycidas," this answer is, when you come right down to it, "That last infirmity of Noble mind"—and he enters this reservation first. Then he briefly develops this limited answer as a form of Stoic ideal, "To scorn delights, and live laborious days." Even that has its limit, however, in death, when the blind Fury "slits the thin-spun life"—just when one is hoping for a blaze of greater renown.

But death isn't a final limit, if you take another way of looking at fame. The other way is shatteringly introduced in the middle of a line that is slipping away into quiet death:

> "But not the praise,"
> *Phoebus* repli'd, and touch'd my trembling ears.

Phoebus *repli'd*, as if to a question, but actually to emphasize the adversative nature of his comment. "Praise" we may think an odd word for Phoebus to use, in view of what follows: it is a word more apt for the favorable response of men than for the affirmative judgment of God. That Milton was content to let it go at that may suggest that he was still not perfectly easy about settling for no recognition on earth.

The actual solution that Phoebus offers is one that denies fame as a human experience and limits it to a divine experience, to the spreading of God's perfect judgment through the agency of pure spirits. And that, says Phoebus, is the kind of fame that can be your true reward in heaven.

We realize in these lines that when Phoebus applies the word "fame" to the earth ("glistering foil," "set off," "broad rumor") it is carrying some of its etymological, neutral sense of "report" (Latin *fama*) rather than the good sense of "renown," and that he is reserving the favorable part for heaven.

Of course this is Phoebus talking, but in his lofty and admired role he could hardly be talking something that Milton disapproved of. And it is interesting to notice that Christ answers Satan to much the same effect that "*Phoebus* repli'd":

> For what is glory but the blaze of fame,
> The people's praise, if always praise unmixt?...
> Th'intelligent among them and the wise
> Are few, and glory scarce of few is rais'd.
> This is true glory and renown, when God
> Looking on th' Earth, with approbation marks
> The just man, and divulges him through Heaven
> To all his Angels, who with true applause
> Recount his praises. (*PR*, III, 47-48, 58-64)

In "Lycidas," the passage on fame ends, thus, with an apparently satisfactory, even ideal resolution of the problem. It is, however, a resolution that conveys a little bit of built-in uneasiness. It is like his resolution to the problem of the inadequacy of his achievements because of that "certaine belatednesse" in him. It makes sense, all right. But can you live with it? That is the deep problem that confronted Milton all of his life—the problem of trying to reconcile logical solutions with his emotional needs.

## IV

There is one other window through which we gain a view of Milton's deep desires. That window is his expression of his fantasies, the stories of what it feels like when he projects himself into unreal situations that free him to express his sincere wishes. There are a number of examples, and I think that their importance has never been recognized for the insight they offer into the private world of his imagination.

They all reveal him brooding on ambition, fame, and immortality. This is the same complex theme which preoccupied him throughout his life and seems never to have been very far below the surface of his consciousness.

The youthful Latin Elegy V ("Anno Aetatis 20") offers at least a clue. In the course of the preamble (11. 9-24), Milton tells of a dream he had. In it, he was swept into the air and carried away to Greece; his mind was separated from his body, and he was seized by the mysterious madness of divine creation. He sees Apollo in the capacity of god of poetry, he is carried through the secret haunts of the poets, he observes all the actions of the gods on Mt. Olympus, and his eyes penetrate the regions of the dead. From this inspiration issued the poem itself, Elegy V, on the coming of spring. The idea was a commonplace one, but for Milton to adapt it into the fantasy of a dream—with his bodiless mind floating through wandering clouds—is significant. At one stroke, he puts himself in the class of true poets and associates himself with the immortality of the gods through poetry.

In his early poems, Milton seems to feel less inhibited when he writes in Latin than when he composes in English. In Latin, he is more inclined to talk of personal matters, or at least less inclined to let conventions of verse stand between him and his own experiences.

The Latin verses addressed to Manso (about 1639) contain a truly remarkable piece of self-revelation in the form of a fantasy. It is open and ingenuous, so irrelevant to the purpose of the poem that the old Marquis must have been either puzzled out of his mind by the passage, or else forced to accept it as an example of the eccentricity of English travelers from the land of "the frozen Bear."

The poem is one of thanks for the kindness and courteous attention shown Milton by Manso in Naples. It takes the slightly odd form of an encomium on Manso for his earlier friendship toward Tasso and Marino. Masso is praised for having taken care of Tasso's remains, for having written a life of Tasso and one of Marino, and for having spread their poetic fame. Thus will Manso have immortality by association with these poets. But,

# The Inner Life

says Milton, what about me? What friend will honor me as a poet, supposing I succeed with the poetry I plan?

Here is where the poem turns into a fantasy and reveals an inner wish that it would doubtless have been difficult for him to articulate in direct address. Milton imagines himself an established poet, famous, old, and dead. He imagines that he has a true friend (as Tasso had Manso) and that the friend is first standing with tears in his eyes beside his deathbed, then depositing his remains in an urn, finally causing a marble statue to be made of him, wreathed with myrtle and laurel in recognition of his poetic achievements. "So I should rest in perfect peace" ("at ego secura pace quiescam"). If all these things could come true, he would look down from Mt. Olympus on the events with serene spirit and peaceful joy.

That was Milton's fantasy (at the age of about 30) of something that would cause him to rest in peace. His fantasy conveys nothing about those hopes for heaven expressed in the resolution reached in the passage in "Lycidas." But it conveys everything about his ambition for fame and immortality as a poet.

In the next year, he had a chance to put that fantasy into practice for somebody else, when (after the death of Charles Diodati) he wrote his "Epitaphium Damonis" (1640). It is his only dramatic poem in which he explicitly presents himself as a fictional character. The spur for the poem is his wish to publish Damon's fame, and to prevent his virtue from going "without a name" and to keep him from being "numbered with the company of the unknown dead" (11. 21-25). Such is the power of poetry that (in Milton's view) Damon's fame will last because of these praises sung by his poet-comrade (11. 28-30, 33-34). (Milton thought it not irrelevant to outline his own poetic plans and to lament that his decision to write in English would limit his own fame to the British Isles [11. 162-78].) So could Diodati, made immortal in poetry, rest in peace. Milton's own fantasy of wishing to have a friend stand by his deathbed with tears in his eyes is echoed in his own wish that he might have stood by Diodati's deathbed,

43

touched his right hand and closed his eyes as he died, and said "Farewell! remember me in your flight to the stars."

Some rare people, on the other hand, can create immortal fame for themselves. The principal fancy of the lines "On Shakespeare" (1630) turns on the idea that Shakespeare was so remarkable that he could create his own immortal monument; unlike Tasso's need of Manso, unlike Diodati's need of Milton, Shakespeare didn't require anyone else to erect a monument or statue, or to provide the needed sepulchre. However they are created, the symbols of immortal fame are all needed.

Bits and pieces of Milton's fantasy about fame through poetry recur in his writings. In the lines "To John Rouse" (1647), he talks only half-jokingly about being made immortal through the deposit of his book in the Bodleian Library, delightful groves of the Muses, divine home of Phoebus, where he will be read along with the sublime writers of classical antiquity. "Lycidas" is Milton's effort to confer immortality on Edward King through poetry, and the glorious flower passage (11. 132-164) is a substitute deathbed scene, with the imaginary flowers summoned up to cover the hearse that isn't there; Milton brings the poem home to himself by imagining that he is dead and by wishing that a poet will favor him likewise when his remains lie in their urn (11. 19-22).

The soaring invocation to Book VII of *Paradise Lost* repeats, with a difference, the motif (as in Elegy V) of flying high above Mt. Olympus, in search of inspiration to create poetry. The flights are risky—the myth of Bellerophon's sky rides on Pegasus is cited in both passages—and there is relief in returning to the security of the ordinary situation.

Flying high above the earth in dreams is a recurrent motif in Milton. Eve's dream about being tempted with the forbidden fruit (*PL*, V, 29-94)—which she describes in the form of a seduction scene—is a notable example. After tasting the fruit, she flies up to the clouds and is, in exhaltation, high above the immense earth stretched out below her. Adam also flies high in the air over Eden in a dream (*PL*, VIII, 292-311); from above, Adam sees the

# The Inner Life

loaded trees, which he wants to pluck and eat. This is the notable occasion when he awakes and finds his dream true. Whatever else all of these scenes of high flying signify, they are all associated with a state of euphoria or (as Milton has Eve say) "this high exhaltation."

To return to earth, Manoa's plan for honoring his dead son (*Samson Agonistes*, 11. 1728-44) is a fantasy relevant to Milton's own desires, and I will mention it as a final example. The plan is remarkably like the kind of honor that Milton had fantasized for himself in the poem to Manso. Friends will gather to do Samson honor, a monument to him will be built, it will be planted with laurel and palm, and his deeds will be commemorated in poetry. Even the virgins will gather (as in "Epitaphium Damonis") to memorialize him with flowers. Thus will immortal fame be assured.

Dreams and visions appear frequently in Milton, and many of them reveal important features of his way of thinking.[4] What we

4. Milton was undoubtedly aware of the large space given to dreams in Herodotus, where dreams have a prophetic character.

Some other examples of dreams and visions in Milton that are important but not directly relevant to a discussion of his inner drives are the following.

In *Comus*, the Lady has a thousand fantasies "of calling shapes and beck'ning shadows dire" (11. 205-20) which she is able to dispel by her "pure-ey'd Faith." The Elder Brother delivers a learned discourse on dreams (11. 457-75), including the way in which "clear dream and solemn vision" convey needed information from "heav'nly habitants" and preserve the pure soul. The Attendant Spirit has something like a fantasy or vision (11. 543-67) which portrays the Lady's danger and animates him to run to her relief.

In *Paradise Lost*, Adam goes into a dream trance from the strain of talking with God (VIII, 460-90) and sees God create Eve, awaking to find her (as he had seen her "in my dream") surpassingly beautiful. Eve has a gentle dream from God (XII, 594-623) which calms her about their expulsion and makes her willing to leave Eden.

In *Paradise Regained*, Christ has a long dream about food (II, 260-301); then Satan appears and tempts him with food, making the table vanish (II, 337-77). Satan so disturbed Christ's sleep "with ugly dreams" of storms, ghosts, and threatening furies that Christ "slept in vain" (IV, 407-26).

The last sonnet, "Methought I saw my late espoused Saint," is Milton's report of a dream vision he had, no matter which wife (if either) it is a report on.

In "Ad Patrem," Milton reports (11. 13-16) that his means consist of what Clio has given him and "the fruit of dreams in a remote cavern and of the laurel groves of the sacred wood and of the shadows of Parnassus."

45

# John Milton

learn about Milton's inner drives from his fantasies is, mainly, that he had a very strong (and unsatisfied) need for recognition. His hopes centered on the possibility of fame–and even immortality–coming to him as a poet. His religious hopes do not feature in an important way in his fantasies.

* * *

Fantasy involves self-dramatization, and there is yet another form of it that recurs through Milton's prose. That is his practice of adopting a persona through which to speak and, sometimes, of implying a dramatic situation.

*Christian Doctrine* is an obvious example. Its salutation demands attention. "John Milton / Englishman / To All the Churches of Christ and to All in any part of the world who profess the Christian Faith, Peace, Knowledge of the Truth, and Eternal Salvation in God the Father and in our Lord Jesus Christ." This salutation (with statement of author, identification of author, and audience) is strikingly similar to the beginning of most of St. Paul's Epistles. The Epistle to the Ephesians, for example, which begins (in the King James version): "Paul, an apostle of Jesus Christ by the will of God, To the saints which are at Ephesus, and to the faithful in Christ Jesus: Grace be to you, and peace, from God our Father, and from the Lord Jesus Christ." (The language is similar, of course, in the salutations to the Romans, I and II Corinthians, Galatians, Ephesians, Philippians, Colossians, I and II Thessalonians, I and II Timothy, Titus, and Philemon, but not much like the salutations in the epistles attributed to those other than St. Paul.) Milton undoubtedly wrote the beginning of *Christian Doctrine* as an allusion to the Epistles of St. Paul. By consequence, he put his book in comparison with those Epistles, and he put himself (as a writer on Christian doctrine) in comparison with St. Paul (the original epistoler of Christian doctrine). The parallel gives Milton the role of an apostle to (as he said) "All the Churches of Christ, and to All in any part of the world who profess the Christian Faith," as St. Paul was an apostle to the various churches of God in his world (Rome, Corinth, Galatia, Ephesus,

46

# The Inner Life

Philippi, Colossae, Thessalonia) and to those who professed the Christian faith (such as Timothy, Philemon, Apphia, Archippus). Although Milton did not publish his book—and it was not printed until 150 years after his death—he chose this form of self-dramatization, which suggests a degree of fantasy in the implied situation.

A good many of Milton's prose works are cast in the form of orations, with Milton as the orator. The clearest example is doubtless the one announced on its titlepage as *Areopagitica; A Speech of Mr. John Milton For the Liberty of Vnlicenc'd Printing, To the Parlament of England*. It is cast in the form of a classical oration, and it uses the expression "Lords and Commons" as a vocative address throughout. The consequence is that a little sense of the imaginary dramatic situation works through the conventional form of the oration and adds urgency to the plea.

Milton addressed some of his other pamphlets of the early 1640s to Parliament. *The Doctrine and Discipline of Divorce* is specifically addressed "To the Parlament of England, with the Assembly," the opening is to the "Renowned Parlament, select Assembly," they are "Lords and Commons" or "Worthies," and the preface is in the form of a letter signed by Milton. In *Reason of Church-Government* it is only in the conclusion that Milton turns to the form of a direct address to Parliament; then he addresses them as "Lords and Commons," "worthy Peeres and Commons," and "yee Lords."[5]

Milton began early to use this style of direct address. In his Cambridge academic exercises, he usually incorporated in the prolusions an address to his supposed audience, presumably under the Latin sway of the vocative case. He also began, in the prolusions, his practice of rather inflating the circumstances by

5. A number of Milton's late pamphlets are also addressed to Parliament, such as *Treatise of Civil Power* (1659) and *The Likeliest Means* (1659). In these he had some reason to hope that they would in fact be read by members of Parliament and would have an effect on the course of political events. They do not, therefore, suggest such an element of fantasy in the self-dramatization as do the earlier ones.

the terms of the rudimentary dramatization; in Prolusions I, II, and VII, he names his audience as "Members of the University," which is true but a somewhat enlarged form of the reality of fellow undergraduates of Christ's College.

Throughout his life, Milton does seem to have retained some sense of elevation very like fantasy in thinking of the audiences for his prose pamphlets. In the *Second Defence* (1654), he gives a candid account of his own sense of the audience that he had addressed in his *First Defence* (1651), and that he is now addressing in this one:

> I have in the *First Defence* spoken out and shall in the *Second* speak again to the entire assembly and council of all the most influential men, cities, and nations everywhere. I seem now to have embarked on a journey and to be surveying from on high far-flung regions and territories across the sea, faces numberless and unknown, sentiments in complete agreement with mine.... Wherever liberal sentiment, wherever freedom, or wherever magnanimity either prudently conceals or openly proclaims itself, there some in silence approve, others openly cast their votes, some make haste to applaud, others, conquered at last by the truth, acknowledge themselves my captives.
>
> Now, surrounded by such great throngs, from the Pillars of Hercules all the way to the farthest boundaries of Father Liber, I seem to be leading home again everywhere in the world, after a vast space of time, Liberty herself, so long expelled and exiled. And, like Triptolemus of old, I seem to introduce to the nations of the earth a product from my own country, but one far more excellent than that of Ceres. In short, it is the renewed cultivation of freedom and civic life that I disseminate throughout cities, kingdoms, and nations. (*Prose*, IV, 554-56)

What Milton imagines here is larger than life, bigger than reality. His audience is all the most powerful people of the world. He—John Milton—has a message of crucial importance for them.

# The Inner Life

They are persuaded by his message, and they capitulate in approval and applause. What he imagines is, actually, very similar to the dream in Elegy V, of being carried away high in the air to Greece. It is also in tune with the invocation to Book VII of *Paradise Lost*, in which he flies high above Mt. Olympus. In all cases, he is a great success, a winner.

Milton's fantasies reveal his inner wishes. Those wishes turn out to reflect his dissatisfaction with the limited recognition he had and with his strong desire for fame. A mighty obligation has been laid upon him, and he must fulfill it. But he has to resort to fantasy to do so.

# Chapter III
## The Sense of the Self

### SELF-ESTEEM

THE KIND OF REGARD we have for ourselves has a fundamental effect on all that we think and all that we do. Milton's sense of self-esteem can, if we understand it fairly, help us to appreciate a good many features of his behavior and of his writing.

An inquiry into such a topic requires caution, however. It is not usually given to us to be able to understand, with much sense of confidence, how others think about themselves. Even the estimates we have of ourselves are almost always oblique or elusive, and sometimes hidden away or disguised. But Milton was much more straightforward than most of us in his measures of himself, and he was clear about the importance of inner drives that are usually observable only indirectly. The unusual degree of his straightforwardness may lead us (if we are not careful) to a harsher judgment of him than the facts warrant.

When he came to write, in the *Christian Doctrine*, about the special virtues connected with the duty of man toward himself (Book II, chapter IX; *Prose*, VI, 724-37), he first dealt with the "virtues which regulate our appetite for external advantages... either to the pleasures of the flesh or to the material possessions and distinctions of our life." But he reserved a special place, after that, for "the appropriate virtues" that obtain "where the distinctions of public life are concerned." From the examples, I judge that he meant not simply kings and rulers and public figures but all prominent people of high talent, including persons like John Milton.

51

# John Milton

These virtues are only two in number and both of them involve inner drives. He calls one of them "humility" ("lowliness of mind" in the first translation), and he calls the other "high-mindedness" ("magnanimity" in the first translation).

"Humility," he says, "gives a man a modest opinion of himself and prevents him from blowing his own trumpet, except when it is really called-for." (A welcome saving clause!) His list of qualities opposed to humility is limited to arrogance, a vain desire for glory, boastfulness, "a crafty or hypocritical playing down of one's own merit, when one is really fishing for compliments," and priding oneself upon one's crimes and misdeeds. Allied to humility is the desire for a good reputation and the approval of good men, with its opposites of shameless neglect of reputation and "an over-eager pursuit of popularity and of praise, regardless of its source."

"High-mindedness is shown," he says, "when in seeking or not seeking riches, advantages or honors, in avoiding them or accepting them, a man behaves himself as befits his own dignity, rightly understood." (Again, that useful final phrase.) Allied to high-mindedness is "indignation when praise or honor are given to those unworthy of them, or when such people enjoy prosperity," and opposed to it are ambition, pride ("when a man is more puffed up than he ought to be, with no or with insufficient justification, or because of some trifling circumstance"), and faint-heartedness.

In setting down these special virtues and their corresponding vices, I do not mean to prepare the case for a judgment of Milton according to his own standards. Under such a court procedure and with a dauntless judge, very few persons of upright views shall scape whipping. I do mean to draw attention to what Milton thought the chief virtues are for man in his duty toward himself. Those virtues, as Milton saw them, are characterized by an emphasis on interior human behavior. That side of life includes our attitudes, our intentions, and our motives—the very qualities that are obscure to the outside observer (and often to the inside occupant as well), and that are most easily misunderstood.

# The Inner Life

Since these are the kinds of topics that I will discuss in this chapter, it will be useful to keep in mind Milton's own ideas, from the *Christian Doctrine*, as background and standard. I will first try to outline Milton's sense of self-esteem as it appears in his extended autobiographical accounts. I will then review some of his more casual self-examinations, look at certain passages in his writings that may tell us of his self-estimates indirectly through their tone, and finally consider some of his ways of dealing with failure.

There is a problem about how we should understand the quotations that I give from Milton's prose. Most of them are drawn from pamphlets written in the seventeenth-century traditions of oratory or polemics, and it is, of course, necessary to keep in mind the differences between those traditions and our own as we try to come to terms with what Milton is saying about himself. Those traditions in the mode of controversy normally allowed a strong claim by the speaker or writer for his own merits, a slashing attack on the adversary, and a spirited defense and counter-attack, with more regard for victory than for the fairness of the details used. It is within this tradition that we must try to distinguish what is individual to Milton from what was expected in the genre of public controversy.

## I

Milton's first extended account of himself appears in *Reason of Church-Government*. This account (the first section of the Second Book, occupying what is available for text in some twenty-three pages of the *Prose*, I, 801-23) gives his explanation as to why he spent his time writing this pamphlet. He did so reluctantly, he says, since all seeking after knowledge and truth is painful, and he did not do it in search of fame or glory.

This controversial prose isn't his kind of writing, he says, as he is actually a poet. He tells of his education, his training, and the praise he received in Italy and at home as a promising poet. He outlines his writing plans in detail, with the different forms he might try—the epic, tragedy, and lyric poetry—with comments on the greatest writers of each, the subjects he might treat in each type, and the rules he might follow. Writing should be for the greater glory of God and for increasing the virtue of the people; it would be well if the minds of all citizens were, on many occasions, ennobled by virtuous writing. It is his efforts along these lines that he is interrupting in order to write this pamphlet.

The overall impact of this eloquent passage is that of high idealism concerning the power of poetry, and a profound desire on Milton's part to become a poet of great achievement in order to contribute to the glory of God and the virtue and well-being of the public. The three great ideals which I discussed in the first chapter are thus epitomized in this single passage.

The passage reveals a learned man who is preoccupied with poetry, with fine examples of each of the recognized forms, with its history and its craft. It reveals a man with a strong, idealistic ambition. For Miltonists, the passage is full of plums—phrases and sentences so well known that they have become familiar quotations.

There is another side to this self-estimate, however. First, it should be noted that this "digression" (as Milton called it) is altogether gratuitous. No one had asked him to explain why he became a pamphleteer, no one had criticized him for not sticking to poetry, and no one had sought an exposition of his prospects in the field of poetry.

I believe it would be fair to say that Milton wrote this long passage because he wanted recognition for himself, and the genre permitted it. It was for the same reasons, I suppose, that his name was, for the first time, placed on the title page—"By Mr. *John Milton.*" Why not? He was thirty-three years old, and the world was not beating a path to his door.

Here, in the form of a permissible digression, was the chance to tell about himself. He felt apologetic about thrusting himself forward, but since it is the kind of thing that men have gotten away with by simply doing it and then quickly making a voluntary confession, he hopes that he can do the same and the cour-

teous reader will pardon him. "Though I shall be foolish in saying more to this purpose, yet since it will be such a folly, as wisest
men going about to commit, have only confest and so committed,
I may trust with more reason, because with more folly to have
courteous pardon." It would be more excusable for a poet to write
of himself, and yet Milton (as a prose writer this time) offers "to
venture and divulge unusual things of my selfe, I shall petition to
the gentler sort, it may not be envy to me" (I, 808).

It is clear that Milton's estimate of himself is, basically, that he
is a poet of very great talent and promise. And of course he was
quite right. The references to Homer, Virgil, Tasso, Sophocles,
Euripides, Pindar, and the others are implied comparisons
between himself and those who had the kind of success he might
achieve; and the glorious eloquence describing the role of the poet
in society represents his personal hopes too. After these
references and this eloquence about his own aspirations as a poet,
he says, "I trust hereby to make it manifest with what small
willingness I endure to interrupt the pursuit of no lesse hopes
then these, and leave a calme and pleasing solitarynes fed with
cherful and confident thoughts, to imbark in a troubl'd sea of
noises and hoars disputes" (I, 821). This sturdy estimate of his
sense of his own importance is also borne out by many smaller
details in the passage.[1]

1. Here are several examples:
Milton's claim that he didn't enter the ministry because he was "Church-
outed by the Prelats" (I, 823) suggests some individual, personal action taken
against him (which was of course not the case) and therefore a greater prominence for himself than he actually possessed. A more accurate (though less
catchy) statement would have been: "I disliked prelatical episcopacy and early
decided not to take holy orders."
Milton clears his motives on the ethical front. He denies writing for "vain
glory" or "praise" (I, 806-07), which are the opposites of the desirable "humility" and "high-mindedness" as he later categorized them in the *Christiun
Doctrine*.
He associates the praise given him in Italy with "some trifles which I had in
memory, compos'd at under twenty or thereabout" (I, 809) and thus inflates the
praise by minimizing its object, like that deplorable "crafty or hypocritical playing down of one's own merit, when one is really fishing for compliments."

# John Milton

If Milton wanted attention, he soon got it. He was attacked in a scurrilous pamphlet called *A Modest Confutation of a Slanderous Libell, Entituled, Animadversions etc.* Milton's *Animadversions* had appeared anonymously in 1641. Although the author of *A Modest Confutation* apparently didn't know who had written the *Animadversions*, that ignorance did not prevent him from making an abusive attack on the bad habits and the weak moral character of the unknown author.

For Milton, the part of wisdom would doubtless have been to remain silent. Instead, he answered in slashing kind in *An Apology Against a Pamphlet Call'd A Modest Confutation* (1642), devoting about eight of its fifty-eight pages to a defense of himself. Milton responded especially to the charge that he had been "vomited out thence" from the University, to the comment that "where my morning haunts are he wisses not," and to the charge that he spent the afternoons "in Playhouses and the Bordelloes."

Milton's response was within the bounds of the tradition of controversy, perhaps on the extravagant side. He always responded when attacked if the occasion permitted. And he was always sensitive to criticism, except for the one instance, from Diodati.

The particular charges that he chose to answer in this pamphlet are worth noting, though we cannot tell what sensitive nerve they touched. His horror at the charge that he was "vomited out thence" from Cambridge may reflect his memory of rustication, or the bad time he had with a tutor. His elaborate answer about his "morning haunts" included full details about what time he got up, summer and winter, his reading habits, and his exercise to maintain a healthy body; this answer suggests a touch of self-righteousness about his habits, or else anxiety that he might somehow fall into that despicable condition of sloth. His answer in abomination of brothels is so excessive and so needless as to make one wonder whether he was afraid of his own sensual impulses.

Finally, he concludes that "if my name and outward demeanour be not evident anough to defend me, I must make tryall, if the discovery of my inmost thoughts can" (*Prose*, I, 889). Those "inmost thoughts" turn out to be, not a trip to the secret places of his mind and spirit, but an account of his education and reading. In an important sense, that reading was a key to, or perhaps almost was, his "inmost thoughts."

Those thoughts reach a glorious climax in that familiar, eloquent association of the poet with virtue: "That he who would not be frustrate of his hope to write well hereafter in laudable things, ought him selfe to bee a true Poem" (I, 890). So long as Milton had the strength of this ideal to support him, his sense of self-esteem was adequate.

Milton's longest account of himself, and his most explicit self-estimate, is contained in his *Second Defence*. When he wrote this pamphlet, he was probably at the peak of his political power and esteem. He knew the leaders who made up the Council of State. His personal role was as a writer-assistant, at a level of prominence comparable, perhaps, to that of a speech writer for a political leader in our times. He had no authority in any of the processes of decision making.

There is much more that one would like to know about Milton's relations with the Council of State and with Cromwell. The evidence is scanty; dedicated Milton scholars, who have searched for ways to give their subject his full deserts, conclude that his role was not important. His influence even on his old friend John Bradshaw (a leader of the Council of State) was apparently limited. Milton's warm recommendation to him (by letter and in person) of Andrew Marvell for appointment as Milton's assistant when a vacancy occurred in the secretariat was not accepted; instead, a younger (and, we would think, less qualified) man was chosen.

To review the essential background of the *Second Defence*. Milton had earlier written his *First Defence* against a pamphlet by Salmasius, a well-known scholar. The *Second Defence* is a reply to a pamphlet which Milton insisted on believing was by the moderately well-known Alexander Morus, though it was actually by an obscure Anglican divine, Peter Du Moulin. The pamphlets

and the answers are full of personal attack on the real (or supposed) authors, in a common polemical style. The Council of
State ordered "That Mr. Milton do prepare something in answer
to the book of Salmasius, and when he hath done it bring it to the
Council" (Parker, p. 369), and Milton said that he also wrote the
*Second Defence* at the request of the Council; he was plainly free,
however, to choose his own time, method, and objective.

We can be grateful that Milton felt the need, in his *Second
Defence*, to reply to the attacks on him. Because in so doing he
gave us the most explicit account we have from his hand of his life
up to that time, when he was over forty-five years old. His story
of his life is recorded in fourteen pages of this account, but the
spirit of his self-estimate runs through the entire pamphlet.

Milton gives, on the whole, a manly, straightforward account
of his life. It is clear that he regards himself as someone quite
special, and he is careful to name the prominent people who have
paid attention to him. His pamphlets are, in his report, rather
more systematic and rather more influential than scholars now
think that they were. There is, for example, a good deal of self-
importance implied in his remark that "I wrote...the
*Areopagitica*, concerning freedom of the press, that the judgment
of truth and falsehood, what should be printed and what suppressed, ought not to be in the hands of a few men (and these
mostly ignorant and of vulgar discernment) charged with the
inspection of books, at whose will or whim virtually everyone is
prevented from publishing aught that surpasses the understanding of the mob" (*Prose*, IV, 625-26). The implied claim that he
had, by that pamphlet, eliminated censorship of the press can be
understood in part—but only in part—as the kind of inflated assertion expected in controversial prose.

Throughout the pamphlet there are a good many evidences
that Milton thought well of himself. The title he gave to this
defence against the attack of an anonymous writer (like the titles
of many of his contemporaries) puts it at a high elevation: *Joannis
Miltoni Angli Pro Populo Anglicano Defensio Secunda*. (The previous

# The Inner Life

pamphlet, against Salmasius, had been similarly entitled: *Joannis Miltoni Angli Pro Populo Anglicano Defensio.*)

Milton took quite seriously his self-imposed role of Defender of the English People. His running figure is of two Knights engaged in single combat. He cries out in a loud voice:

> It was I and no other who was deemed equal to a foe of such repute and to the task of speaking on so great a theme, and who received from the very liberators of my country this role, which was offered spontaneously with universal consent, the task of publicly defending (if anyone ever did) the cause of the English people and thus of Liberty herself. Lastly, I thank God that in an affair so arduous and so charged with expectation, I did not disappoint the hope or the judgment of my countrymen about me, nor fail to satisfy a host of foreigners, men of learning and experience, for by God's grace I so routed my audacious foe that he fled, broken in spirit and reputation. (*Prose*, IV, 549)

He engages himself, not as a private Knight, but on behalf of his country. "For who," says Milton, "does not consider the glorious achievements of his country as his own?" (*Prose*, IV, 550). And who is there who does not try to live up to what he thinks his role to be?

> To no one, even the humblest, do I willingly compare myself, nor do I say one word about myself in arrogance, but whenever I allow my mind to dwell upon this cause, the noblest and most renowned of all, and upon the glorious task of defending the very defenders, a task assigned me by their own vote and decision, I confess that I can scarcely restrain myself from loftier and bolder flights than are permissible in this exordium, and from the search for a more exalted manner of expression. (*Prose*, IV, 553-54)

"That Mr. Milton do prepare something in answer," or words to that effect, has become a general mandate, with "universal consent," that makes him swell in anticipation.

# John Milton

He proceeds, with a deep bow to the need for humility and high-mindedness:

> In the degree that the distinguished orators of ancient times undoubtedly surpass me, both in their eloquence and in their style (especially in a foreign tongue, which I must of necessity use, and often to my own dissatisfaction), in that same degree shall I outstrip all the orators of every age in the grandeur of my subject and my theme. (*Prose*, IV, 554)

The occasion is so sublime that it induces a self-vision of such epic proportions in Milton's mind that it deserves another look, in addition to my earlier reference:

> This circumstance has aroused so much anticipation and notoriety that I do not now feel that I am surrounded, in the Forum or on the Rostra, by one people alone, whether Roman or Athenian, but that, with virtually all of Europe attentive, in session, and passing judgment, I have in the *First Defence* spoken out and shall in the *Second* speak again to the entire assembly and council of all the most influential men, cities, and nations everywhere. I seem now to have embarked on a journey and to be surveying from on high far-flung regions and territories across the sea, faces numberless and unknown, sentiments in complete agreement with mine. (*Prose*, IV, 554-55)

Milton has the world at his feet, and the people are hanging on his words. (He is indulging himself in a controversial tactic, to be sure, but he is going beyond any usual measure.) His account rolls on for almost two hundred more words, in commendation of the Germans, the French, the Spaniards, and the Italians, at last lapping the shores of the Indian Ocean in joy that "it is the renewed cultivation of freedom and civic life that I disseminate throughout cities, kingdoms, and nations," even unto the uttermost parts of the earth.

The polemical nature of the pamphlet encouraged some revelations of Milton's estimate of himself. Let me allude to several which are especially illuminating:

# The Inner Life

• His repetition of the claim that the sharpness of his *First Defence* was perhaps responsible for the death of Salmasius.

• His tireless adulation of Queen Christina of Sweden for her "nice discernment" in changing her mind about (and, in effect, discarding) Salmasius after reading his *First Defence*.

• His advice to Cromwell as to who should be the next three persons selected for the Council of State—his advice was not followed—and an admonition about freedom of the press, as from an elder statesman to a novice ("May you permit those who wish to engage in free inquiry to publish their findings at their own peril without the private inspection of any petty magistrate," *Prose*, IV, 679).

• His self-congratulation on having described the conditions of true liberty and his warning to the English people that the perpetuation of it is now their responsibility.

Political pamphlets of the seventeenth century are not the place to look for modesty. In this rough-and-tumble context, Milton naturally overvalued his prominence and his importance as a political writer, and seems to have taken full advantage of this opportunity to describe his own merits and achievements.

## II

Milton set a high standard for himself, as I have already suggested, and he stuck to that kind of expectation throughout his life. "Nothing common or mediocre can be tolerated," as I quoted him as writing in the Seventh Prolusion; and in the *Apology* he said, "Last of all, not in time, but as perfection is last."

In *Christian Doctrine*, he lays it down that our aim should in fact be perfection: "As for perfection, although it is not to be hoped for in this life, we ought nevertheless to struggle and strive towards perfection as our ultimate goal" (*Prose*, VI, 482). Thus in Milton's view our ultimate goal is not stated in religious terms of fulfilling God's will, or of uniting our selves with God in love, but in moral terms of "perfection."

In theory, Milton felt that it was unwise to set too high a standard for yourself by being unduly scrupulous about details. On

61

# John Milton

one occasion, he went so far as to say that it is actually dangerous to imagine obligations and to repress human impulses. In an important perception, he suggested that undue repression could result in some undesirable manifestation, either outward or inward:

> Let not therfore the frailty of man goe on thus inventing needlesse troubles to it self to groan under the fals imagination of a strictnes never impos'd from above, enjoyning that for duty which is an impossible and vain supererogating. *Bee not righteous overmuch*, is the counsel of *Ecclesiastes; why shouldst thou destroy thy self?* Let us not be thus over-curious to strain at *atoms*, and yet to stop every vent and cranny of permissive liberty: lest nature wanting those needful pores, and breathing places which God hath not debarr'd our weaknes, either suddenly break out into some wide rupture of open vice, and frantick heresy, or els inwardly fester with repining and blasphemous thoughts, under an unreasonable and fruitles rigor of unwarranted law. (*Doctrine and Discipline of Divorce, Prose*, II, 354)

About repression as the cause of religious fanaticism, Milton took a view interestingly similar to that of *A Tale of A Tub*, though not of course in Swift's vein. Milton suggested that religious fanatics may

> be such most commonly as are by nature addicted to a zeal of Religion, of life also not debausht, and that their opinions having full swinge, do end in satisfaction of the flesh, it may come with reason into the thoughts of a wise man, whether all this proceed not partly, if not cheefly, from the restraint of some lawfull liberty, which ought to be giv'n men, and is deny'd them. As by Physick we learn in menstruous bodies, where natures current hath been stopt, that the suffocation and upward forcing of some lower part, affects the head and inward sense with dotage and idle fancies. (*Doctrine and Discipline of Divorce, Prose*, II, 278-79)

# The Inner Life

It would doubtless have been healthier for Milton if he could have given himself more "needful pores, and breathing places." He did not break out in open vice or frantic heresy, nor (so far as we know) did he fester with repining and blasphemous thoughts. And he stuck with the high standards for himself.

It is my impression that Milton was thoughtful about himself but not deeply introspective; he does not report, at least, that he brooded over his faults in trying to live by his standards. He himself felt that he was sometimes, in fact, a little too inclined to self-examination.[2]

His most notable account of self-examination occurs in the *Second Defence*, when he is answering the allegation that his blindness is God's punishment on him for his earlier writing:

> I call upon Thee, my God, who knowest my inmost mind and all my thoughts, to witness that (although I have repeatedly examined myself on this point as earnestly as I could, and have searched all the corners of my life) I am conscious of nothing, or of no deed, either recent or remote, whose wickedness could justly occasion or invite upon me this supreme misfortune.... I likewise call God to witness that I have written nothing of such kind that I was not then and am not now convinced that it was right and true and pleasing to God. And I swear that my conduct was not influenced by ambition, gain, or glory, but solely by considerations of duty, honor, and devotion to my country. (*Prose*, IV, 587)

It is noteworthy that Milton discovered no serious offense as a result of his grave self-examination and visit to all the recesses of his heart; but we must still remember that he was writing a polemical pamphlet.

---

2. "For if I be either by disposition, or what other cause too inquisitive, or suspitious of my self and mine own doings, who can help it?" (*Reason of Church-Government*, *Prose*, I, 804). Or, in the letter of about 1633 to an unknown friend, "I am something suspicious of my selfe" (*Works*, XII, 325).

# John Milton

Milton goes further in his self-examination and reports on those drives that lie behind action. He tells of his motives in his political pamphleteering: he wrote not out of ambition, or for money, or for glory, but because of his sense of duty, grace, and devotion to his country. This account is more like an expression of hope that he has not only clean hands but also a pure heart.

Milton was sensitive about criticism. He bridled, in *Defence of Himself*, at Alexander Morus's suggestion that he had praised himself; he was, however, able to acknowledge his merits by attributing them to the sources of his values.

> I have never praised myself; nor, as you charge, will you ever find a panegyric pronounced by me upon myself. Singular indeed is the favor of God toward me, that He has called me above all others to the defence of liberty, a cause which has been so bravely vindicated; and I confess that this favor I have acknowledged (nor should it ever go unacknowledged) and that I took thence the noble matter of my exordium, which, as I think, is in no way blameworthy.
>
> (*Prose*, IV, 735)

In fact, Milton seemed to be able to hear praise of himself even when it was faint or a long way off. His understanding of his fame as a pamphleteer can perhaps be summed up by the concluding lines from Sonnet XXII (To Cyriack Skinner) when he explains what supports him in his blindness:

> Yet I argue not
> Against heav'n's hand or will, nor bate a jot
> Of heart or hope; but still bear up and steer
> Right onward. What supports me, dost thou ask?
> The conscience, Friend, to have lost them overplied
> In liberty's defense, my noble task,
> Of which all Europe talks from side to side.
> This thought might lead me through the world's
> vain mask
> Content though blind, had I no better guide.

# The Inner Life

It is "liberty's defense, my noble task" that animates him—"of which all Europe talks [or, perhaps, if you favor the Phillips version "rings"] from side to side." Here he is not writing within the tradition of public controversy. The consistency of what he says in this sonnet with his claims in his pamphlets tends to confirm that we have been in touch with Milton's true feelings about himself.

His foreword (in Latin) to the conventional eulogies about him that were included in his 1645 *Poems* is in a similar vein. He claims, in conclusion, that "he is seeking with might and main to fend off from himself the odium that excessive praise begets, and prefers that he should not be credited with more than is his due, he can not, in the meantime, deny that he sees a signal honor to himself in the favorable judgment of men of intellect reinforced by high distinction" (*Works*, I, 155).

Fame can give power. Sonnet VIII (When the Assault Was Intended to the City)—though it is probably a playful poem—promises that he can perpetuate the name of the person who is good enough to spare his house. He, who can be compared with Pindar and Euripides, "can spread thy Name o'er Lands and Seas, / Whatever clime the Sun's bright circle warms."

A good name has to be watched over vigilantly, however. Even in the last year of his life, Milton was ready to spring to his own defense when he thought he had been attacked. The anonymous author of *The Transproser Rehears'd* (1673) included some sharp, vicious remarks about Milton in his pamphlet. The old Milton, after thirteen years of silence on the pamphleteering front, promptly dictated to an amanuensis a reply in which he attacked the nameless writer. Milton's answer was not published, however, and it has never come to light (Parker, pp. 629-30).

## III

The word "I" is of the first importance in Milton's prose. And so is the concept for which it stands. Examples abound throughout his writings. We must, once again, be careful to adjust our

# John Milton

understanding of his words in the light of the seventeenth-century traditions of oratory and controversy.

Here are a couple of examples from his undergraduate years. "If there is any room for an insignificant person like myself, Members of the University"—so he begins Prolusion II "after you have heard so many eminent speakers, I too will attempt, to the best of my small powers, to show my appreciation of this day's appointed celebrations, and to follow, though at a distance, the festal train of eloquence to-day" (*Prose*, I, 234). Or this portion of his ceremonial preparations for the kick-off of Prolusion VI: "I would before all have you know that I have not spoken thus in a spirit of boastfulness. For I only wish that such a stream of honeyed, or rather nectared, eloquence might be granted me, if but for this once, as of old ever steeped and as it were celestially bedewed the great minds of Athens and of Rome" (*Prose*, I, 269).

It was of course conventional to assert a low self-estimate, but such statements come easiest to those who are eager to be asked to move to a higher place at the table. I believe that Milton never thought himself "insignificant" or possessed of only "small powers." Likewise, his denial of boasting—a frequent denial of his—concerning his powers of eloquence is another oratorical convention and perhaps an appeal to his hearers to move him up a place or two.

One of Milton's favorite tactics for beginning an essay is to explain how he happened to write it. The Preface to *Eikonoklastes*, for example, first tells the reader that he is not writing out of "fond ambition, or the vanity to get a Name." He is, in fact, reluctant to write: "I take it on me as a work assign'd rather, then by me chos'n or affected. Which was the cause both of beginning it so late, and finishing it so leasurely, in the midst of other imployments and diversions" (*Prose*, III, 337, 339).

By putting himself first, he seems to be supposing that the reader wants first to know the motives of that "J.M." named on the title page before he knows anything else. One would think that the first and central issue is: what is this book about and what is its main message. But no: Milton puts himself first. And he

# The Inner Life

increases his own importance by letting his "other imployments and diversions" take precedence over the writing of this book.

Sometimes Milton comes forward in his own person to give force to his declarations. In the *Defence of Himself* he imagines himself as the prosecutor of Alexander Morus—another one of his fantasies—and brings him (with a cloud of witnesses) before the bar of eternal justice on behalf of himself, and on behalf of the people of England: "In my own name, and in the name of the English people...I deliver you, More,...into the judgment of all the ages" (*Prose*, IV, 766-67). There are two signatories to the complaint: John Milton, and the People of England. It is a nice touch to put the two in parallel.

Sometimes the texture of the language is all that is needed to reveal the importance that Milton attached to himself in the course of his writing. Consider the following passage from *Of Civil Power*, being Milton's address to Parliament, particularly the emphasis that falls on the "I":

> Of civil libertie I have written heretofore by the appointment, and not without the approbation of civil power: of Christian liberty I write now; which others long since having don with all freedom under heathen emperors, I should do wrong to suspect, that I now shall with less under Christian governors, and such especially as profess openly thir defence of Christian libertie; although I write this not otherwise appointed or induc'd then by an inward perswasion of the Christian dutie which I may usefully discharge herin to the common Lord and Master of us all, and the certain hope of his approbation, first and chiefest to be sought: In the hand of whose providence I remain, praying all success and good event on your publick councels to the defence of true religion and our civil rights.
>
> John Milton (*Prose*, VII, 240)

The three actors in this passage are God, Milton, and Parliament, and Milton's rhetoric conveys his sense of his own importance. His last pamphlets are particularly forthright in calling attention

# John Milton

to the favor he has had from God and the protection he has enjoyed from Parliament.[3]

Sometimes the "I" can be important without even appearing. It never appears, for example, in "The Verse"–the prefatory statement that the printer got Milton to write (along with the Argument) for the 1668 reissue of *Paradise Lost*. And yet this short essay conveys a great deal about Milton's sense of self-esteem entirely through the tone of the passage. It should be read as a modest example within the genre of Renaissance literary criticism, in which the tone of clear affirmation was generally strong.

The little essay is a defense of the lack of rhyme in *Paradise Lost*, and the opening sentence sets the tone: "The measure is *English* Heroic Verse without Rime, as that of *Homer* in *Greek*, and of *Virgil* in *Latin*." A quick definition, with two parallels, blunt and direct, built on the implied dichotomy of *Rhyme/Lack of Rhyme.*

A kind of debate is then set up between *Rhyme* and *Lack of Rhyme*. The main mode of the debate is attack, and the principal device is the association of value terms with each. Consider the value terms that are used to attack *Rhyme:*

- "no necessary Adjunct or true Ornament of Poem or good Verse"
- "the invention of a barbarous Age, to set off wretched matter and lame Meter"

---

3. *Likeliest Means to Remove Hirelings out of the Church* is a good example, with such passages as the following, in which the rhetorically permissible flattery becomes both a persuasive and a self-inflater: "Owing to your protection, supream Senat, this libertie of writing which I have us'd these 18 years on all occasions to assert the just rights and freedoms both of church and state, and so far approv'd, as to have bin trusted with the representment and defence of your actions to all Christendom against an adversarie of no mean repute, to whom should I address what I still publish on the same argument, but to you whose magnanimous councels first opend and unbound the age from a double bondage under prelatical and regal tyrannie; above our own hopes heartning us to look up at last like men and Christians from the slavish dejection, wherin from father to son we were bred up and taught; and thereby deserving of these nations, if they be not barbarously ingrateful, to be acknowledgd, next under God, the authors and best patrons of religious and civil libertie, that ever these Ilands brought forth" (*Prose*, VII, 274).

# The Inner Life

- "trivial and of no true musical delight"
- "the jingling sound of like endings"
- "the troublesome and modern bondage."

On the positive side, here is the principal value term associated with *Lack of Rhyme:*

- "to be esteem'd an example set, the first in *English*, of ancient liberty recover'd to Heroic Poem."

The debate is also carried on by associating appropriate *Writers* and *Readers* with *Rhyme* and with *Lack of Rhyme*. The *Writers* associated with *Lack of Rhyme* are Homer, Virgil, "both *Italian* and *Spanish* Poets of prime note," and "our best *English* tragedies"; with *Rhyme* are associated writers of "a barbarous Age" and "some famous modern Poets" who used rhyme "much to thir own vexation, hindrance, and constraint to express many things otherwise, and for the most part worse than else they would have exprest them." Finally, the *Readers* associated with *Lack of Rhyme* are "all judicious ears," while those associated with *Rhyme* are "vulgar Readers."

Literary theory is thus converted into polemics, and the tactics of controversy are employed. If you can get by with this kind of rhetoric, how can you lose a debate? The tone will not win friends, however, at least among the spirited. As the author of *The Censure of the Rota* told Milton, "You fight always with the flat of your hand like a rhetorician, and never contract the logical fist." The tone of "The Verse" is, I think, superior, uncompromising, and belligerent in establishing its position through attack. Toward those who might be disposed to think otherwise, it is unkind, even contemptuous.[4]

There were doubtless reasons beyond the conventions of Renaissance literary criticism which could in part explain the tone: Milton may have resented the printer's request, he may have been working off his feelings against rhymers, he may have felt

4. An interesting parallel to Milton's little essay is the last verse paragraph of Andrew Marvell's dedicatory poem to the second edition of *Paradise Lost*. Marvell, too, makes fun of "tinkling Rime" in comparison with Milton's verse; but there is a world of difference between the tones.

69

grouchy that day. We don't know. We do know that this is what he allowed to be printed and reprinted. And we do know that the tone is very familiar to those who have read his controversial prose with attention. I conclude that there is a good deal of Milton's sense of self-esteem in this passage.

## IV

Milton did not always gain the goals that he set for himself. To put it in a more human way: like everyone else, Milton sometimes failed. Sometimes the failure may have been the result of his own act or omission; sometimes the failure may have been thrust upon him. Mostly we don't know enough to explain the reasons for the failures.

His marriage to Mary Powell was, for whatever reason, a disastrous failure for three long years. His four divorce tracts failed in their effort to change laws or customs or attitudes: they mainly brought him a measure of ill repute. His anti-prelatical tracts caused no changes in ecclesiastical practices. The effects of his political pamphlets are hard to assess; at best, the results were rather modest, and in the eyes of his time he was irrefutably on the losing side.

If we focus on one short period in which his efforts were intense and concentrated, we can perhaps gain a clearer understanding of one of the various kinds of failure with which Milton had to come to terms, time and again. Consider the months of the composition of his political pamphlets in 1659, when he threw himself wholeheartedly into the enterprise of trying to prevent the Restoration.

In December of 1658, he began work on a pamphlet of advice to Parliament arguing that it is unlawful for civil magistrates to use force in matters of religion. The pamphlet, of ninety-six pages, was completed and registered in February 1659 and published under the title *A Treatise of Civil power in Ecclasiastical causes: Shewing that it is not lawful for any power on earth to compel in matters of Religion*. It had no discernible effect. Milton turned then to write a somewhat longer pamphlet of advice to Parliament on the reformation of the clergy, particularly by eliminating government payment to ministers. It was completed and published in August 1659 under the title *Considerations Touching the Likeliest Means to Remove Hirelings out of the church. Wherein is also discoursed Of Tithes, Church-fees, Church-revenues; And whether any maintenance of ministers can be settl'd by law.* Again, no results. Events were moving rapidly, and Milton tried to move with them. It was clear that sentiment was building up in favor of the return to kingship. And so Milton devoted himself to writing a tract against kingship. He called it *The Ready & Easie Way to Establish a Free Commonwealth, and the Excellence therof Compar'd with the inconveniences and dangers of readmitting kingship in this nation.* It was published in March 1660, and it was greeted with scornful laughter. As negotiations with Charles II became more open, Milton worked even faster. He rewrote and enlarged his pamphlet and in little more than a month a second edition was issued; "revis'd and augmented," says the title page, "The author J. M." and "Printed for the Author." But the new edition was out only shortly before all possibility of its influence was at an end. The king returned in triumph in May 1660. Milton's efforts were in vain.

The witty author of *The Censure of the Rota upon Mr Milton's Book entitled The Ready and Easy Way to Establish a Free Commonwealth* (1660) dealt a sharp blow to Milton. He asked why Milton "did not give over writing, since" he had "always done it to little or no purpose." In all candor, there was much truth to the charge (Parker, p. 560).

He had suffered failures before, and there were still more ahead of him. His efforts to prevent censorship of the press—on which he set such store—came to nothing in his lifetime. In 1662, universal censorship of the press was re-established. In the same year, the ecclesiastical freedom to which Milton had devoted so much of his attention was severely limited. The Act of Uniformity required all clergymen, university professors and other university officials, and schoolmasters and private tutors to renounce the Solemn League and Covenant and accept the liturgy of the Established Church.

# John Milton

The principles underlying the positions that Milton took on such issues as these have all been gradually adopted in democratic societies. But not until long after he was dead. Later, people could say, "He was far ahead of his time! He was a prophet!" But such sayings would be too late to help his self-esteem. During his lifetime, his political efforts seemed to result in total failure.

Then there is the crucial issue of his fame as a poet—the matter that was of such deep importance to him in his system of values and as the object of his inner drives. It seems to be a sad truth that his contemporary reputation as a poet was very limited. He did not get the fame that he so badly wanted. The talent for poetry that he was sure he possessed thus was not validated by any reasonable form of public recognition. A few noteworthy persons acknowledged his genius soon. Andrew Marvell, to be sure, in his splendid dedicatory lines to the second edition of *Paradise Lost*, and John Dryden's remarkable epigram which joined Milton with Homer and Virgil little more than a decade after Milton's death. But general fame was not for Milton to enjoy. Fame had to be the work of aftertimes.

I have mentioned a series of instances in which Milton might be said to have failed in reaching his objective. These are not casual or unimportant cases. They are related to his most important goals. Other persons might describe these instances in different ways, and some might very well think that other examples were more appropriate. But I believe that the central proposition is clear: Milton had to put up with a lot of failure.

The key question is this. How did he cope with failure? The answer may reveal a great deal about him. One thing that he did not do was to acknowledge failure. For example, in his writings he never made any explanatory comment of this nature touching those three years when his bride deserted him and refused to come back. In his writings, he never faced the fact that his pamphlets did not really succeed in the way that he had hoped they would. We have no recorded comment of his recognition that he did not achieve the fame as a poet that he devoutly hoped for.

# The Inner Life

How was he able to manage? In the first place, he had an almost incomparable amount of determination. This quality is allied to that drive to work harder and longer than anybody else in order to try to achieve his goals. His fixed beliefs in his ideals never deviated, so far as one can tell.

When he did not succeed in his expectations, he did not take refuge in any of those indirect ways of self-purification. He did not resort to some substitute satisfaction and claim it was what he had sought in the first place. He did not transfer the blame to other persons and complain that they were responsible for his failures. Nor did he blame the world at large and become sour or embittered or misanthropic in his outlook.

What he did seems to me a remarkable achievement of single-mindedness and will, however reluctant one might be to follow that path. Personally, I believe that he was aided by the possession of an unusual self-distancing quality, one that tended to neutralize the damaging effect of high emotions by pushing them in the direction of impersonality.[5]

What does all this mean? I think it means, among other things, that Milton simply could not face failure. He had that extraor-

---

5. This quality is evident, I think, in the abundance of wit and irony throughout a large part of his writing. I believe that the accepted view runs more in the direction of making fun of the elephant wreathing his lithe proboscis and gravely agreeing that Milton was no good at carving cherry stones. Since this is not an appropriate place to argue a case that would require much space to present fairly, I have to content myself with alluding to a few characteristic examples of Milton's wit in his verse: the Hobson poems, Sonnet XI, To John Rouse, On the Engraver of His Likeness, and Sonnet VIII.

For a couple of typical examples from his prose: in *Areopagitica*, the passage about the five imprimaturs ducking their shaven reverences to one another (*Prose*, II, 504) or the marvellous absurdities he suggests to regulate all recreations and pastimes as natural extensions of licensing (II, 523-30); or, in the *Second Defence*, Milton's wonderful flight of fancy as to the topics on which Salmasius might have been lecturing to the maidservant in the garden shed rather than seducing her (IV, 565-67).

Parker alludes frequently and persuasively to Milton's wit; see the entries under "humour" and "wit" in his index.

dinarily high sense of values and that exceedingly (even compulsively) strong drive to live up to them. His sense of self-esteem required him not to fail in his endeavors, even though they might be beyond his powers in the circumstances in which he found himself, or that he chose, or into which he was forced. Still, he could not fail. He must not. And so, in his own conscious view, doubtless he did not.

Every distorted view of reality puts a strain on the viewer. He must keep disparate views from destroying one another, or (sometimes) even the stability of their possessor. Milton managed very successfully, perhaps even magnificently, under this kind of strain.

His adjustment involved him in some positions that may strike us as being incompatible with the idea of a hero. So be it. One is his frequent, almost constant, overvaluation of his role in the political arena, and of his own importance as a government spokesman. Or, to mention one small example that has embarrassed Milton lovers, his willingness to publish the incomplete "Passion" for our edification even though it wasn't good enough to suit him. ("This Subject the Author finding to be above the years he had, when he wrote it, and nothing satisfied with what was begun, left it unfinisht.")

In the course of writing poetry, Milton probably got rid of a good many of the emotions that were hard for him to manage. I assume that he was often, without necessarily knowing it, drawn to his subjects and to the portrayal of emotions by his own need for expression. We can only guess about this, it is true.

Milton and Samson have a remarkable amount in common: blind men of mature years, among enemies, failures in their high mission, and the rest. So do Milton and Satan, as rebels and revolutionaries. And so do Milton and Christ, as virtuous and high-principled persons. Everyone can go on and on and add examples. *Paradise Lost* and *Paradise Regained* and *Samson Agonistes* are all anatomies of failure mixed in with success, and of success mixed in with failure. Milton's writing about the failures of others may have been the only way available to him of recognizing his own failures.

I do not for a moment suggest that we would do well to study Milton's poetry to learn literal facts about his life. Of all the forms of literary study, that is among the most unrewarding. I do suggest that Milton probably worked off some of his difficult emotions in his poetry. And some of those emotions would have had to do with his own frustration at not being able to live up to what he expected of himself.

I first thought of using, as an epigraph for this chapter, the following plea by Milton: "Do not then, whoever you are, hastily accuse me of arrogance." I did not do so because I thought it might cast a shadow of misunderstanding over the chapter. Also, the quotation would have been wrenched out of its time and place. It occurs in the First Prolusion (*Prose*, I, 224), written in Milton's undergraduate years at Cambridge, presumably early; it is the beginning of his admission that he is modifying the mythology of classical poets.

I quote it now for its symbolic value. I think that it is relevant as a plea for understanding by readers of Milton today. It is not a plea to ask us to see Milton without his flaws. Rather, it is a plea to recognize that his values and his inner drives and his sense of self-esteem were all exceedingly complex, sometimes in conflict with one another, not always entirely reconciled. And to be fully aware that the sense of Milton's self cannot be readily summed up nor fairly comprehended within the scope of any single term.

# Chapter IV
## The Sense of Others

How we look on others depends, first of all, on how we look on ourselves. Milton's sense of other persons is a kind of mirror held up to himself. It shows something of his capacity for awareness of others, and something of his limitations. It may sometimes enlarge or distort his needs and fears, but it gives an essential insight into his inner life. As with all of us, that inner life may be one that its possessor is unwilling or unable to face himself, much less knowingly reveal it to others. He was speaking for many people when he wrote, in the Seventh Prolusion, that "the chief part of human happiness is derived from the society of one's fellows and the formation of friendships" (*Prose*, I, 295). It is a question as to whether it proved true for him.

Milton's sense of other persons developed and changed in the course of his life, though some of the central points remained more or less fixed. From what he wrote on the subject at different times, we may draw several different conclusions. Some of his comments are so memorable that we may be tempted to take any one of several as a fair epitome of his entire field of vision. For example:

> still govern thou my Song,
> *Urania*, and fit audience find, though few.
> But drive far off the barbarous dissonance
> Of *Bacchus* and his Revellers.

These lines from the Invocation to Book VII of *Paradise Lost* express contempt for the mob and admiration for the elite, and they are a true summary of his feelings at that time about masses of people. They do not reveal the complexity of his feelings about other individuals as friends or acquaintances, nor the social road he traveled; and those matters are important to an understanding of Milton's inner life.

Let me offer, first of all, an outline of the facts about the family background that had a shaping influence on his outlook toward other persons. Then I will review his early experiences in trying to form relations with others and his thoughts on friendship. I will discuss the nature and the significance of the one true friendship that Milton had in his early manhood. From that point, I will review the social nature of the rest of his life and his attitudes toward others. Finally, I will discuss the social dynamics of his dramatic poems in search of patterns of behavior to see what they mean and how they are related to what we otherwise know of Milton's sense of others.

## I

Milton's childhood appears to have been somewhat limited in human relationships. When Milton was born, his father was about forty-six years old and his mother about thirty-six. They had already had several children (we do not know how many), but only one, Anne, had survived infancy (and we do not know how old she was when Milton was born). Milton was thus the first son of a couple who would have been, in their times, middle aged, or even approaching elderliness when he was a child. Seven years after Milton's birth, they had one more child, a son, Christopher, when the father was fifty-three and the mother about forty-three.

Milton's earliest years were thus spent in the regular company of an older sister and a relatively elderly mother, in addition to the servants of the household of a moderately well to do businessman, and with his father—and older man, professional scrivener, amateur musician—whenever he was at home.

Almost nothing is known of Milton's relations with his mother.

# The Inner Life

On the one occasion in his writings when he mentioned her, in the *Second Defence*, in telling "who I am, then, and whence I come," he says only that she was "a woman of purest reputation, celebrated throughout the neighborhood for her acts of charity" (*Prose*, IV, 612)—not a very stirring testimonial of a son about his mother. Other sources add nothing of value toward an understanding of their relations.[1] Milton does include her (by saying "parents") in his explanation of the several forces which had formed his original plan to become a minister in the established Church, "to whose service by the intentions of my parents and friends I was destin'd of a child, and in mine own resolutions."[2]

Milton's remarks about his father are more extensive. "My father was a man of supreme integrity," he wrote in the *Second Defence*, and this summation should be compared with the parallel comments I have just quoted about his mother. It is illuminating to single out the further references to his father in the same passage about himself. "My father destined me in early childhood

---

1. There are three other early sources of information about her. Edward Phillips describes her (his grandmother) as "a woman of incomparable virtue and goodness"; the anonymous biographer says that she was "a prudent, virtuous wife"; and John Aubrey adds the homely detail of her weak eyes and her need for glasses after the age of thirty.

2. *Reason of Church-Government*, 1641 (*Prose*, I, 822). These are intentions of which we hear no more, beyond the remainder of the passage, in which Milton tells of giving over this intention after he had come "to some maturity of yeers" and had perceived "what tyranny had invaded the Church" and was "thus Church-outed by the Prelats." The original intention to enter the ministry has, in my opinion, been greatly overemphasized as a crucial feature of Milton's life, and this rather vague passage has been made to carry the heavy burden of a variety of inferences and unsupported particularities. Parker, for example, lays great stress on it, and recurs to it again and again; in his index, under *Ministry, Milton's dedication to the*, there are twenty-five separate entries. The passages in his biography referred to range in value from misleading to wrong. I quote the first as an example; Parker is reporting the reaction of the parents to the birth of Milton on December 9, 1608: "To his devout, middle-aged parents Christmas was a memorable season in that year. Unto them a son was born. Gratefully, they dedicated their child to God's ministry" (p. 6). Let me repeat: the only basis for this unfounded assertion—and for Parker's other twenty-four passages on the subject—is the single vague sentence I quoted in the text.

for the study of literature.... My father took care that I should be instructed daily both in school and under other masters at home. When I had thus become proficient in various languages and had tested by no means superficially the sweetness of philosophy, he sent me to Cambridge, one of our two universities.... I returned home.... At my father's country place, whither he had retired to spend his declining years, I devoted myself entirely to the study of Greek and Latin writers.... When I had occupied five years in this fashion, I became desirous, my mother having died, of seeing foreign parts, especially Italy, and with my father's consent I set forth, accompanied by a single attendant" (IV, 613-14).[3]

These references to his father have a respectful, deferential tone, while his mother is allowed to expire in an ablative absolute. His allusions to his father suit a figure whose actions and whose attitudes carry high and unquestioned authority with Milton. He adopted that tone of respect and deference very infrequently in his writings throughout the course of his whole life. Respect for the father was more likely to receive public acknowledgement in the seventeenth century than respect for the more private role of the mother, of course, but Milton carried this common practice about as far as it can go.

Milton's autobiographical account continues from the time of his departure for Italy (with his father's consent, and one attendant), in 1638, when he was nearly thirty, on to 1654 (when he was approximately forty-six). But it is worth noting that his father is never mentioned again. His account of himself after his return from Italy reflects a new view, with a greater focus on himself. I "rented a house in town, sufficiently commodious for myself and my books," he writes, "and there, blissfully enough, devoted myself to my interrupted studies" (IV, 621), and so on.

3. Milton had earlier expressed pleasure in visiting "his father's house." In 1626 he answered Diodati's letter about being exiled from Cambridge by saying, "But if this be exile, to have returned to the paternal home and to be carefree to enjoy a delightful leisure, then I have no objection to the name or to the lot of a fugitive and I am glad to take advantage of my banishment" (Elegy I, 11. 17-20).

# The Inner Life

Nothing more of his father or of his father's house, but a greater sense of his own self-sufficiency.

Milton's mother had died in 1637, the year before he went to Italy. When he returned to London and rented his commodious house, he was financially independent—though only modestly so—by virtue of the income from investments made by his father and given to him. Milton's father was living with the other son, Christopher, and his family in Reading; but in 1643, after the surrender of Reading, his father apparently came to live with Milton in London. He was then eighty or eighty-one. So far as we know, he continued with Milton until he died in 1647, at the remarkable age of eighty-five.

Many things happened to Milton during those four years—reunion with his separated wife, birth of his first child, harboring various family members in time of civil strife, publication of half a dozen important pamphlets and his first volume of collected poems which included the first appearance in print of a very significant poem addressed to his father. But we know nothing of the part of Milton's father in these momentous events, nor of his reaction to them. All we know is Edward Phillips' remark that he was "wholly retired to his rest and devotion, without the least trouble imaginable." Milton himself was totally silent about his father during those years and thereafter, except for the passage to which I have already referred.

There is special poignance in the absence of reaction on the part of his father to the 1645 *Poems*. That volume was the first major fulfillment of Milton's promised career as a poet, a career which had developed much more slowly than he wished it had done. At last, at the age of thirty-seven, a book of his poems was published.

He had described something of that proposed career to his father in the poem which he entitled "Ad Patrem." That remarkable Latin poem conveys an open-hearted expression of gratitude from a loving son to a respected father. What is of most significance is the spirit of the poem: the spirit of cordial friendliness, of sincere appreciation, of joy in his own role, of devotion toward a

81

loved one. It is a kind of ideal thank-you poem from a grateful son to a father for all the good things that have come to the son. It is remarkable for its manliness, its sincerity, and its lack of affectation. It suggests a rich and deep relationship between father and son, as only such a relationship could (I think) make possible such a poem as this one is.

It is true that the poem also suggests that the musician father had made some kind of slighting remark about poetry, and the son offers an affectionate, personal argument in the hope of changing his father's mind about poetry as a sister art to music: "Phoebus himself, wishing to part himself between us two, gave some gifts to me and others to my father; and, father and son, we share the possession of the divided god" (64-66). It is impossible to know what the father had said, and whether it wounded Milton's sense of self-esteem. The objection came from the source with the greatest potential impact on him, from a father whom he admired and respected and loved for both traditional and personal reasons. My guess, from a careful reading of the poem (and its conclusion in particular), is that Milton did not take the objection as a threat to his essential identity, which was (it is true) closely tied up with fulfilling the role of poet. But the main point is that the poem—written sometime between 1631 and 1645, for this purpose it doesn't much matter when—shows that Milton had, as a young man, a warm sense of human relationship with his father. And that is a truly important fact about John Milton.[4]

4. Those who know "Ad Patrem" mainly from the scholarship on the poem may be surprised by how I choose to describe its central importance. The largest body of scholarship has dealt with the date of its composition, and the text has been tossed and gored—in the absence of any shred of external evidence, aside from its date of publication—in an effort to find some support for a date from internal evidence; we are just about as far from knowing the date with certainty now as we were before. Parker, who is wonderfully helpful on so much of Milton, is very nearly at his worst on this poem; his pages on it (pp. 125-28, 788-89) are a spiderweb of speculation and irrelevance. I believe that a good deal of the usual understanding of the poem comes from reliance on an English translation that is blunt and direct rather than (as I read the Latin) graceful and full of sensibility. For one tiny example: *despice* (1. 17) is ordinarily translated as *despise*, though a juster reading would be *look down on* or *disparage*.

# The Inner Life

Before proceeding with a review of how Milton's relations developed when he went into the world outside of his family, I would like to record his own estimate of his essential personality. He had "a certain reserv'dnesse of naturall disposition," he wrote, and "a certaine niceness of nature, an honest haughtinesse, and self-esteem either of what I was, or what I might be, (which let envie call pride) and lastly that modesty, whereof though not in the Title page yet here I may be excus'd to make some beseeming profession..." (*Apology against a Pamphlet, Prose,* I, 892, 890).

This was in 1642, and he was defending himself against attack. Moreoever, he could tell only what he was aware of and what he could allow himself to see and to describe. But, so far as it goes, this self-description seems to be exemplified in his behavior at about that time. How precisely accurate it was then, or earlier, or later, we have no other way of knowing. Milton was, in his own view, in 1642, a man of natural reserve, fastidious, haughty, and with a sense of self-esteem. As the younger version of such a man, and with the family background I have outlined, he ventured forth into the world of men and women.

## II

Parents we have thrust upon us, but we may choose our friends. Milton's early search for friends involved him in some awkwardness and some blundering. There is not much evidence about his friendships of pre-college years, but we can learn a great deal about his sense of others from the academic exercises that he wrote while an undergraduate at Cambridge.

Of the seven academic exercises—or prolusions—that have been preserved, four contain specific clues about his relations with his fellow undergraduates: about how he felt toward them, about how he tried to gain their approval. As the academic exercises were mainly written on assigned topics as demonstrations of mastery of the forms of persuasion, they have to be approached with a certain wariness, not forgetting that they are, first of all, display

83

pieces in the art of rhetoric. The practice of extracting assertions from the prolusions and presenting those assertions, out of their context and ignoring their purpose, as Milton's essential ideas can sometimes be misleading.

They were delivered orally, in Latin, as oratorical performances–either in Christ's College or in the University Public Schools–and an important feature of most of them is Milton's sense of relation with his audience of fellow undergraduates. The tone and spirit give a clue. In the first two, he is hostile, contentious, and ill at ease; in the third, he is hortatory and superior, like someone who is sure that he knows more than his listeners do; in the fourth and fifth, he is engaging, friendly, less cocksure; in the sixth, he is self-consciously engaging to the point of obsequiousness; and in the seventh, he is serious, self-confident, straightforward, idealistic, superior, in the role of leader. The order of their composition cannot be proved, but it seems a reasonable assumption that the order of their first printing is the order of their composition. They appeared in 1674, in the year of Milton's death, at the instigation of the printer, who in his Preface expressed the refreshingly candid hope that they would be "saleable (which is my chief personal concern)."

Throughout the prolusions, Milton expresses a desire to gain the good will of his audience or to please them. This result is a necessity for the success of his exercise, as he is frank to admit;[5] and his other expressions of a like desire–"my consuming desire and longing to please you"[6]–in the last two prolusions are prob-

5. "...the speaker must begin by winning the good-will of his audience; without it he cannot make any impression upon them, nor succeed as he would wish in his cause" (First Prolusion, *Prose*, I, 218). "I have been deeply occupied of late, gentlemen, in seeking, and indeed one of my chief anxieties has been to find, what device of rhetoric would best enable me to engage my hearers' attention" (Third Prolusion, *Prose*, I, 240).

6. Sixth Prolusion (*Prose*, I, 270); or "nothing could give me greater pleasure and satisfaction than your presence here, than this eager crowd in cap and gown, or than the honourable office of speaker..." (Seventh Prolusion, *Prose*, I, 288).

ably to be understood in a rhetorical more than in a personal vein. Several passages in the prolusions have a crucial importance for us in understanding the development of Milton's relations with others, and I hope that readers will think more about the development than about the language he used on one or another of the occasions.

In the first prolusion, Milton portrays himself as one who feels that his fellow students dislike him. "How can I hope for your good will," he says, "when in all this great assembly I encounter none but hostile glances, so that my task seems to be to placate the implacable? So provocative of animosity, even in the home of learning, is the rivalry of those who pursue different studies or whose opinions differ concerning the studies they pursue in common" (*Prose*, I, 219).[7]

This prolusion is not an impromptu performance but a speech prepared in advance; hence the comment about encountering "none but hostile glances" reflects Milton's expectations. He seeks their goodwill for professional rather than personal reasons, he says: that is, he wants to be successful in his exercise and he knows (according to approved doctrine) that his first task is to create goodwill. In saying this, he reveals himself as goal-oriented, not person-oriented. He is irritated to have his assignment made difficult, and he is peeved at his audience for causing him trouble. If he actually thought—as he later said—that this rough opening would make the audience more friendly, he didn't (at least at that time) know the way people usually react to such treatment.

He goes on to admit (or claim) that a few in the audience are friendly to him. He warms to those few, but bitterly attacks the majority. This tactic, which may have been planned to arouse

7. With reluctance, I quote the translation used in *Prose*, by Phyllis B. Tillyard. It is a puzzle to me as to why this translation should have been adopted, almost universally. To me, it is lacking in the spirit, vivacity, and idiom of the original. In many important passages, the translation by Bromley Smith in *Works* seems clearly superior.

pity or friendliness toward the underdog, is actually more likely to strengthen dislike:

> Yet to prevent complete despair, I see here and there, if I do not mistake, some who without a word show clearly by their looks how well they wish me. The approval of these, few though they be, is more precious to me than that of the countless hosts of the ignorant, who lack all intelligence, reasoning power, and sound judgment, and who pride themselves on the ridiculous effervescing froth of their verbiage.

One would think that these round assertions of general condemnation would suffice. But no. Milton warms to the task of showing his aptitude for *inventio* and flails these "hosts of the ignorant" with cudgels drawn from classical antiquity and natural philosophy.

> Stripped of their covering of patches borrowed from new-fangled authors, they will prove to have no more in them than a serpent's slough, and once they have come to the end of their stock of phrases and platitudes you will find them unable to utter so much as a syllable, as dumb as the frogs of Seriphus. How difficult even Heraclitus would find it, were he still alive, to keep a straight face at the sight of these speechifiers (if I may call them so without offence), first grandly spouting their lines in the tragic part of Euripides' Orestes, or as the mad Hercules in his dying agony, and then, their slender stock of phrases exhausted and their glory all gone, drawing in their horns and crawling off like snails. (*Prose*, I, 220)

Doubtless this burst of *elocutio* was satisfying to the speaker, less satisfying to the audience under attack. Even this early, Milton has the feeling that only a few favor him and the multitude is against him. This feeling was, whatever the facts, doubtless an expression of his wish to be more popular than he thought himself to be. His tactic, both on a rhetorical and a personal level, is an effort to achieve that condition. The response of attack may sometimes work in a rhetorical exercise, particularly as *refutatio*, but it rarely works in human relations. In the human sense, Milton is off on the wrong track, and he makes himself into an elitist in an assumed posture of self-defense, as one against many.

After having laid about him and cudgeled the crowd, he then proceeds to offer them a treaty of peace. But it is more like a temporary truce to criminals, offered on the condition that the malefactors will promise to listen to him sympathetically:

> If there is anyone who has refused peace on any terms and declared war *à mort* against me, I will for once stoop to beg and entreat him to lay aside his animosity for a moment and show himself an unbiassed judge in this debate, and not to allow the speaker's fault (if such there be) to prejudice the best and most deserving of causes. If you consider that I have spoken with too much sharpness and bitterness, I confess that I have done so intentionally, for I wish the beginning of my speech to resemble the first gleam of dawn, which presages the fairest day when overcast. (*Prose*, I, 220-21)

This begging is of a rather superior nature, and the thought of having been at fault is mentioned as if it were a remote possibility. And the figure of the sunrise could hardly excuse the bitter denunciations, except to the proud producer of them.

The first prolusion–in summary–shows Milton, the undergraduate, at his worst in human relations. It suggests a person who badly wants approval and friendship but who doesn't know how to merit them.

In the third prolusion, Milton changes his tactics radically. The same audience is now addressed as "men so erudite in every branch of learning," and of himself he says of pleasing that "I greatly fear it is beyond my poor abilities, yet it shall be my chief wish to afford this also: but even if I attain this, it will not be enough unless I succeed also in persuading you." He turned to rhetoric for help. "Rhetoric, again, so captivates the minds of men and draws them after it so gently enchained that it has the power now of moving them to pity, now of inciting them to hatred, now of arousing them to warlike valour, now of inspiring them beyond the fear of death" (*Prose*, I, 240, 244). Good classical and Renaissance doctrine indeed, to which the spirits of Aristotle and Cicero and all of Milton's other favorites would rise in assent!

Though Milton's praise of rhetoric may have been a formality in this exercise, it turned out that this attitude points to a central fact in Milton's belief about human relations. That was his deep belief in rhetoric, in the power of masterfully arranged words to control human behavior. He exemplifies this belief over and over again in his poetry, and I will examine a few key examples in the last section of this chapter. The failure of this belief to work in his private life was to be the sad cause of much of his disappointment.

In the sixth prolusion, the formal subject is Milton's defense of "sportive exercises," and the occasion called for jests and foolery. But woven into the texture of the exercise are Milton's self-doubts about his relations with others, as well as his ideas about how satisfying relations may be achieved. He comes out from behind the art of rhetoric and (doubtless encouraged by the pleasantry of the occasion) reveals his private feelings. Among the reasons that made him willing to deliver the oration on this occasion, he says, was the friendliness he sensed:

> I was further strongly induced and persuaded to undertake this office by the new-found friendliness towards me of you who are fellow-students of my own college. For when, some months ago, I was to make an academic oration before you, I felt sure that any effort of mine would have but a cold reception from you, and would find in Aeacus or Minos a more lenient judge than in any one of you. But quite contrary to my expectation, contrary indeed to any spark of hope I may have entertained, I heard, or rather I myself felt, that my speech was received with quite unusual

# The Inner Life

applause on every hand, even on the part of those who had previously shown me only hostility and dislike, because of disagreements concerning our studies.

This is a manly admission by Milton of the mistake he had made, presumably in the first prolusion, in his expectation that his fellow students would be hostile to him. He was then on the verge of despair, and he responded with hostility of his own. Now "the new-found friendliness towards me of you who are fellow-students of my own college" releases him from the grip of his hostility.

A generous way indeed of displaying rivalry, and one worthy of a royal nature! For while friendship itself is often wont to misinterpret what is really free from faults, on this occasion keen and biting enmity was kind enough to construe in a more gentle and lenient spirit than I deserved both my mistakes, which may have been many, and my rhetorical failures, which were doubtless not a few. On this one occasion and in this one instance mad fury seemed to become sane, and by this action to free itself from the imputation of lunacy.

Before, Milton likened his fellow students to snails; now they are of a royal nature. Their show of friendliness brings him to admit that there was some basis for their earlier dislike of him. The cloudy skies are beginning to clear.

I am quite overcome with pride and joy at finding myself surrounded on all sides by such an assembly of learned men; and yet, when I take stock of myself and turning my eyes inward contemplate in my own heart the meagre powers I possess, I blush to myself and a sudden uprush of sadness overwhelms and chokes my rising joy.

So great is the power of kindness and friendship! Those whom he had despised as totally ignorant can now be admired as "an assembly of learned men." He no longer has the need to berate the others and rate himself above all the rest; he can even admit

89

his own shortcomings in sincerity rather than (as before) in false modesty.

> But, gentlemen, do not, I beg of you, desert me as I lie here fallen, and stricken by your eyes as by lightning. Let the soft breeze of your goodwill refresh my fainting spirit, as well it can, and warm it into life again; so shall my sickness, thanks to you, be less acute, and the remedy, since it is you who apply it, the more willingly and gladly accepted; so that it would be a true pleasure to me often to faint thus, if I might as often be revived and restored by you.

He throws himself on the mercy of his fellow students. He has enough confidence to expect their continued approbation. And he pays back their approval in advance, in full measure. This recantation converts condemnation to admiration, replaces hostility with friendship. Once underway, he can hardly bring himself to stop.

> But what matchless power, what marvellous virtue is yours, which like Achilles' spear, the gift of Vulcan, at once inflicts the wound and heals it! For the rest, let no one wonder that I triumph, as though exalted to heaven, at finding so many men eminent for their learning, the very flower as it were of the University, gathered together here; for I can scarce believe that a greater number flocked of old to Athens to hear those two supreme orators, Demosthenes and Aeschines, contending for the crown of eloquence, or that such felicity ever fell to the lot of Hortensius at any declamation of his, or that so great a company of cultured men ever graced a speech of Cicero's. So that with however poor success I perform my task, it will yet be no mean honour to me merely to have opened my lips before so large and crowded an assembly of our most eminent men. (*Prose*, I, 267-68)

And so he continues for several more periods, with many flattering remarks to "so polished and refined an audience" as he is addressing. Somehow, it all seems a little too good to be true, and one has a hard time believing in that much of a turnaround by Milton or by his fellows.

Pretty soon Milton is musing on the qualities needed for making friends. "What is more likely," he asks, "to win friendship quickly and retain it long, than a pleasant and gay disposition? while if a man is devoid of wit and humour and elegant pleasantry, hardly anyone will find him agreeable or welcome.... If a man does not desire to be considered cultured and witty, he must not be annoyed if he is called a clown and a boor" (*Prose*, I, 271, 272).

Milton seems to be equating "a pleasant and gay disposition"—the most likely quality to make and retain friendships, he thinks—with the possession of "wit and humour and elegant pleasantry." This is the learned man's equation, emphasizing verbal (rhetorical) qualities in the self without regard for such human qualities of concern for others as helpfulness or quiet listening. It is an equation that seems to have dominated his thinking, at least for some years, as an aspect of his faith in rhetoric.

The approval of his peers was certainly important to him. It is touching to read the terms of his admission: "Finally, gentlemen, I invoke the seal of approval set by yourselves, which I consider worth all the rest" (*Prose*, I, 274).[8] But he feels sufficiently confident of his ground to raise a question that apparently troubled him about his fellow students—the puzzle as to why "some of late called me 'the Lady.'"

This passage is often taken out of its context and therefore misunderstood. One should bear in mind that it is part of this sportive academic exercise, that it does not appear in the more serious, narrative, first part but in the second section, which is supposed

8. The translation known to the many readers of Merritt Hughes's useful edition (and others) is a little more explicit: "Finally, fellow students, I appeal to you for your approval and support, which are worth as much as all the rest to me" (p. 616 A). Or that in *Works:* "Finally, fellow students, I may refer to your own guardianship and patronage, which will be to me worth them all" (XII, 221).

to be principally jests and puns and comments calculated to bring forth laughter from the audience. Milton is making a mild sort of fun of himself and giving himself a chance to ransack the stores of classical antiquity and produce answers that verge on the absurd.

Why have they called him "the Lady"? Because he's not tall? Then how about Demosthenes? Because he hasn't tossed off great bumpers like a prize fighter? Because he doesn't have the rough hands of a plowman? And so on for a page, in a mostly jolly tone.

But not altogether jolly. There is still an underlying sense of puzzlement. Why indeed have they called him "the Lady," rhetorical answers aside? Is it because he really isn't masculine enough to be accepted wholeheartedly by his fellows? Or has he failed in some other way in his effort to make friends? We don't know. What does seem clear is that this passage is usually misinterpreted, overinterpreted, to Milton's detriment.[9] The passage concludes on a friendly, jocular key: "And so I take up my *rôle* of Father [of the festivities] and address myself to my sons, of whom I perceive a goodly number, and I see that the jolly rascals acknowledge me as their father by a furtive nod" (*Prose*, I, 284). Playing with the gender question has set up this joke of the Lady as the Father.

The seventh prolusion has few jokes in it, and the task of defending learning brings out the deep idealism in Milton. He is intent on praising central values, and he even includes himself in his attacks on the shortcomings of undergraduates.

In praising learning as a basis for friendship, he starts with the principle which I quoted at the beginning of this chapter: "The chief part of human happiness is derived from the society of one's

9. There is no help from other contemporary commentary. Aubrey says: "His complexion exceeding fair [he was so faire that they called him the Lady of Christ College]." Anthony à Wood simply repeats this comment. It is worth noticing that Milton doesn't raise the question about his complexion, which would have been an unthreatening explanation; he could doubtless have found apposite references to light or dark complexions in the Greek and Roman classics had he wanted to do so. I am inclined to doubt Aubrey's conclusion that fairness of complexion was the cause of the nickname.

fellows and the formation of friendships." A crucial principle, and one that he is prepared to support ardently and defend wholeheartedly against attack. And with good reason. Right away, he tries to anticipate and answer the objection that learned men are lacking in the qualities which are thought to be important for friendship.

> It is often asserted that the learned are as a rule hard to please, lacking in courtesy, odd in manner, and seldom gifted with the gracious address that wins men's hearts. I admit that a man who is almost entirely absorbed and immersed in study finds it much easier to converse with gods than with men, either because he habitually associates with the gods but is unaccustomed to human affairs and a stranger among them, or because the mind, expanding through constant meditation on things divine and therefore feeling cramped within the narrow limits of the body, is less expert in the nicer formalities of social life. But if such a man once forms a worthy and congenial friendship, there is none who cultivates it more assiduously. (*Prose*, I, 295)

There is, presumably, an element of self-portraiture in this passage, as Milton's great ideal was (as we have seen) to be a learned man. The truly learned man, he argues, may not win friends smoothly and quickly, as he himself did not. Milton is very understanding and gentle (as we are glad to be with ourselves) in explaining that the reasons are not to the discredit of the learned man; "but if such a man once forms a worthy and congenial friendship, there is none who cultivates it more assiduously." And the results are notable.

> For what can we imagine more delightful and happy than those conversations of learned and wise men, such as those which the divine Plato is said often to have held in the shade of that famous plane-tree, conversations which all mankind might well have flocked to hear in spell-bound silence? But gross talk and mutual incitement to indulge in luxury and

lust is the friendship of ignorance, or rather the ignorance of friendship. (*Prose*, I, 295)

Learning is to be defended, and ignorance is to be attacked. The handiest target is undergraduates, and off he goes at their laziness, at their gluttony and drinking (*Prose*, I, 300). He takes some of the sting out of his attack by ostensibly including himself—it is "we" and "our," not simply "you" and "yours"—but it is pretty plain who is to bear the brunt of the attack. Next it is the turn of the teachers, and he is ready to run through the entire curriculum: as to grammar and rhetoric, "one may hear the teachers of them talking sometimes like savages and sometimes like babies"; of logic, "its teachers are not like men at all, but like finches which live on thorns and thistles"; likewise with the current teaching of metaphysics, natural philosophy, mathematics, and jurisprudence: avoid all these irrelevant, superfluous, and unprofitable parts of the arts (*Prose*, I, 300-01).

These observations may be a testimony to Milton's honesty and his idealism. (They represent his continuing convictions, and he is still pushing the same views in 1644 in *Of Education*, when he talks of "our dullest and laziest youth" and of "that asinine feast of sowthistles and brambles which is commonly set before them, as all the food and entertainment of their tenderest and most docile age.") But this blunt tactlessness would probably alienate his listeners and make it all the harder for him to form friendships.

This prolusion includes a hint about one of Milton's predilections which make it easier to understand his difficulty in making friends. He really preferred, at least some of the time, a life of retirement and of seclusion. After telling about his summer vacation "amid rural scenes and woodland solitudes," where he felt that he "had enjoyed a season of growth in a life of seclusion," he goes on to say that "I might indeed have hoped to find here [at Cambridge] also the same opportunity for retirement..." (*Prose*, I, 289). This is not to say that he wanted to be a hermit or to retire from the world of man, but it is to say that (at least at this time, and as a young man) he felt the need for periods of retirement and solitude.

# The Inner Life

## III

If a learned man "once forms a worthy and congenial friendship," we remember Milton writing in the seventh prolusion, "there is none who cultivates it more assiduously." Milton had one such friendship in the years of his young manhood, and that friendship—with Charles Diodati—had a profound influence on him: Diodati's importance to Milton was of the same general magnitude as—though of course different in kind from—that of his father.

Milton and Diodati were schoolmates at St. Paul's School, and about the same age. Diodati went to the other university and died in 1638, when Milton was nearly thirty. The extant writings that record their friendship include two letters by each (Milton's in Latin, Diodati's in Greek), two Latin verse letters from Milton to Diodati (now known as Elegy I and Elegy VI), one sonnet in Italian by Milton to Diodati (now known as Sonnet IV), and Milton's great Latin elegy to Diodati, the "Epitaphium Damonis." Although we know very little about their activities together, it is a fair inference that they saw one another a good deal during the vacation periods and that they went off together on one-day holiday jaunts.

The main evidence about their friendship is in the writings I have mentioned, and the most revealing feature is the attitudes toward each other that their writings convey. Unfortunately, we usually read them in translations which set literal accuracy above attitude, and I hope that readers will re-consult the originals in assessing my personal estimate.

Milton's two verse letters to Diodati are open, friendly, easy, familiar, cordial. They date from Milton's undergraduate years (1626 and 1629, apparently), and they are full of ebullience. In the first, Diodati is "dear friend" ("care"), "a heart that is loving and a head so devoted to me," and Milton pours out his feelings—which we may consider adolescent—about the theater and about the attractive girls he has seen in London. The other one begins with an affectionate response to Diodati: "You would like to be informed by a song how I return your love and how fond I am of you. Believe me, you can hardly learn it from this song, for my love is not confined by narrow meters and it is too sound to use the lame feet of elegy." He writes a bouncing, spirited, good-humored letter about poetry, and ends by telling Diodati about the verses he has just written, the "Nativity Ode"–"and you, when I recite them to you, shall be my judge." Since Milton considered the making of poetry to be his high and noble calling, a judgment on his poetry was a judgment on the essence of his productive life. It is therefore a profound testimonial to the friendship of these two men that Milton should so openly offer to have Diodati be the judge of his poem. I am not aware of any similar invitation by him to any other person about any poem.

The prose letters that they exchanged also convey, first of all, a sense of intimacy. The subjects are sometimes commonplace–planning a holiday, or failing to answer letters promptly–but each of them expresses a deep wish to be with the other. Milton speaks of "the intimacy of our friendship" and opens his heart to Diodati, "even about what I am thinking. Listen, Diodati, but in secret, lest I blush; and let me talk to you grandiloquently for a while. You ask what I am thinking of? So help me God, an immortality of fame. What am I doing? Growing my wings and practising flight." And he proceeds, in this spirit of confidence, to reveal his plans to his friend. But friendship does not run only in one direction. "But what about you?" Milton asks, and wants to share the private plans of his friend.

They share admiration for one another, and Diodati can address Milton as "you, extraordinary man." But he can also go on, in this revealing and important letter, and make critical comments with affection and gaiety about how Milton should change his style of life:

> But you, extraordinary man, why do you despise the gifts of nature? Why such inexcusable perseverance, bending over books and studies day and night? Live, laugh, enjoy your youth and the hours, and stop reading the serious, the light,

# The Inner Life

and the indolent works of ancient wise men, wearing your-self out the while. I, who in all other things am your in-ferior, in this one thing, in knowing the proper limit of la-bor, both seem to myself, and am, your better." (*Prose*, I, 337)

Milton was to be the object of much criticism during his lifetime and afterward–most of it on unjust grounds. But, so far as I know, no one ever again made any critical comments to him with affection.

Because within about a year Diodati was dead, and no one was able to take his place in Milton's heart. A good while had to pass, he tells us, before he comprehended the death of his friend. Then, more than a year after the event, he wrote the "Epi-taphium Damonis"–in my view, a much greater poem than it is usually reckoned.

In the course of pouring out "his tremendous sorrow," Milton muses on the merits of Diodati and on his faith that Diodati will be immortal. But it is also a personal poem, and Milton tells of his personal loss in the death of Diodati.

> But what at last is to become of me? What faithful compan-ion will stay by my side as you always did...? Who now is to beguile my days with conversation and song?... To whom shall I confide my heart? Who will teach me to alle-viate my mordant cares and shorten the long night with delightful conversation...? Who then will bring back to me your mirth and Attic salt, your culture and humor?... Here was grace and here was gentleness. (37-43, 45-47, 55-56, 127)

These questions define the role that Diodati played, in Milton's view, as his friend. All gone. Quite gone.

Since there will hereafter be no one with whom to share mu-tual confidences (to "confide my heart"), Milton uses the poem almost as if it were a verse letter to Diodati. He tells what is prob-ably the greatest confidence he has, his own plan for writing poetry. "I am afraid that I am vain, yet I will relate it," and he goes into the kind of current detail (11. 159-78) that had earlier followed such a remark as "Listen, Diodati, but in secret, lest I blush."

For our present purposes, the crucial part of the poem is the long passage (11. 93-111) on the nature of friendship. It is a passage which is heart-rending in the human context of the poem. It is also absolutely central to an understanding of Milton's sense of others. He begins with a contemplative account of companionship among animals and birds. Animals play and feed together; each bird has a fellow, and each gets another fellow in the case of untimely death. Milton is establishing the solemn contrast with the human condition as he feels it.

> But we men are a painful race, a stock tormented by cruel fate, with minds mutually alienated and hearts discordant. A man can hardly find a comrade for himself in a thousand; or, if one is granted to us by a fate at last not unkind to our prayers, a day and hour when we apprehend nothing snatches him away, leaving an eternal loss to the years.

The Latin has such a solemn severity and such a funereal cadence that it deserves to be quoted as well:

> Nos durum genus, et diris exercita fatis
> Gens, homines, aliena animis, et pectore discors,
> Vix sibi quisque parem de millibus invenit unum,
> Aut, si sors dederit tandem non aspera votis,
> Illum inopina dies, qua non speraveris hora
> Surripit, aeternum linquens in saecula damnum.

This is a passage which is prophetic in relation to Milton's future. It was written, I believe, under great emotional pressure, and it puts the human condition (as Milton conceived it) in the bleak terms that the circumstances brought from him. Milton was, to some degree, of that *durum genus*. While he was perhaps never altogether *aliena animis, et pectore discors*, there was that element in him. And the death of Diodati was a permanent loss

# The Inner Life

*aeternum linquens in saecula damnum.* As the circumstances subsided, the terms would subside too. But the prophecy would continue to carry weight.

## IV

Milton lost Diodati, and he never found another true "comrade." But he did not allow himself to be separated from the world of man. In fact, he lived a richly social life from the time, at the age of about thirty, when he first rented that commodious house in London for himself and his books.

Before his marriage, he used "to drop into the society of some young sparks of his acquaintance...; with these gentlemen he would so far make bold with his body as now and then to keep a gawdy-day" (Edward Phillips).

In the 1640s, his house accommodated his two nephews and (from time to time) several other boys all of whom were his pupils, his father, his wife, her parents and siblings, and his first child. After the initial difficulty between Milton and his wife had been overcome, they apparently had a congenial life together, and three children. When his first wife died, he married a second time, happily, after a lapse of four years. When his second wife died, in childbirth, he married a third time, very happily, after a lapse of five years, and this wife–his "Betty"–survived him.

The Milton home, whichever the house, was an active household, with servants and (after he became blind) people to read to him and take dictation from him. It was a house of music–Milton played his organ and his bass-viol, and he sang–and there were guests for dinner, "with wine." Milton was a pipe smoker and an active conversationalist: he was "of a very cheerful humor" and "extreme pleasant in his conversation, and at dinner, supper, &c. but satirical" (Aubrey): "his deportment was sweet and affable" (the anonymous biographer). In his later years, he suffered greatly from the gout–of which he died at the age of sixty-six, having "been long troubled with that disease, insomuch that his knuckles were all callous, yet was he not ever observed to be very impatient" (the anonymous biographer); "he would be cheerful even in his gout-fits, and sing" (Aubrey).

I believe that Milton was afraid of loneliness. In his divorce tracts, he recurs over and over again to the thought that marriage is intended to prevent or to cure loneliness. The implication is that one may not have many friends and one may find society alien; but marriage is one sure refuge against being alone. "What thing more instituted to the solace and delight of man than marriage?" he writes in the *Doctrine and Discipline of Divorce;* "God in the first ordaining of marriage, taught us to what end he did it, in words expresly implying the apt and cheerfull conversation of man with woman, to comfort and refresh him against the evill of solitary life." Marriage is "the remedy of our lonelinesse," and the disease is greater "if especially his complexion incline him to melancholy" (*Prose*, II, 235, 229, 247).[10] So far as we know, after that false start with Mary Powell, the signs are that he had a congenial family and home life.

Milton had no true "comrade," perhaps, but he had many friends and visitors. He was "frequently visited by persons of quality...; all learned foreigners of note, who could not part out of this city, without giving a visit to a person so eminent; and lastly, by particular friends that had a high esteem for him." "The visits of foreigners" were frequent "almost to his dying day" (Edward Phillips). "He was visited much by learned, more than he did desire.... Foreigners came much to see him, and much admired him....and would see the *house and chamber* where *he* was born. He was much more admired abroad than at home" (Au-

10. The same thought dominates the *Doctrine and Discipline of Divorce*. A few other examples are: In the institution of marriage, God promised "a meet help against loneliness." "*It is not good*, saith he [God], *that man should be alone; I will make him a help meet for him*...in Gods intention a meet and happy conversation is the chiefest and the noblest end of mariage....And the solitarines of man, which God had namely and principally orderd to prevent by mariage, hath no remedy, but lies under a worse condition then the loneliest single life....that same God-forbidd'n lonelines which will in time draw on with it a generall discomfort and dejection of minde....the pining of a sad spirit wedded to lonelines should deserve to be free'd" (*Prose*, II, 240, 245-47, 248).

brey). Although he was not wealthy, "he was not sparing to buy good books, of which he left a fair collection; and was generous in relieving the wants of his friends" (anonymous biographer). Milton's daughter Deborah remembered him as "Delightful Company, the Life of the Conversation" and a man of "Unaffected Chearfulness and Civility" (*Literary Records*, V, 104); a maidservant and her sister recalled Milton as "very merry" (*Literary Records*, V, 218, 222).

In Milton's later years, he had many close friends. The four singled out by Edward Phillips for special mention are Andrew Marvell, Edward Lawrence, Marchamont Needham, and "above all" Cyriack Skinner; these were his special friends, yet they were, on an average, about twenty years younger than he. We know that Milton saw each of them frequently, with cordiality and warmth. These relationships are a remarkable commentary on Milton's attractiveness as a human being and his capacity for friendship. He was an older man, blind, in disfavor. And yet these younger men sought him out and counted him their close friend. There were others as well, and casual little comments, like Dryden's account of a visit with Milton, suggest a large array of acquaintances who valued Milton.

The private letters by and to Milton (beyond the correspondence with Diodati, which I have already discussed) generally support this view of Milton's social nature. In time of trouble, Milton depends on his friends, as he tells Leonard Philaras in 1654: "the signal kindness of Providence" and "the voices and visits of friends" make it easier to bear his blindness (*Prose*, IV, 870).[11] He was grateful when foreigners spent the time to write to him or to look him up. This passage from a letter to Emeric Bigot, in 1657, reveals a good deal about his feelings toward other individuals and toward himself:

11. Milton did not always feel that the darkness of his blindness was that easy to bear, or that the conversations and visits of friends were available to him. In the invocation to Book III of *Paradise Lost*, we can recall his lamentation that he has been "from the cheerful ways of men/cut off."

# John Milton

That on your crossing over to England I seemed to you more worthy than others to seek out and call upon was extremely and naturally gratifying to me; and that you greet me by letter after so long an interval is even more welcome. For though at first you might have been led to me by the opinion of others, you could hardly return now by letter unless drawn back by your own judgment, or at least good will. Thus I surely have reason to congratulate myself. (*Prose*, VII, 497)

It is a graceful, friendly message, but it also reveals Milton's need for reassurance and his pleasure in the approval of others. He goes on: "I am glad therefore that you are convinced of my peace of mind in this severe loss of sight and in my willingness and eagerness to receive foreign guests." *Peace of mind* (or *serenity of spirit*) is the attitude that Milton seems to have conveyed to others, at least during the last twenty or twenty-five years of his life. There were many testimonials to Milton from foreign and domestic sources, none perhaps more touching than that by Peter Heimbach on June 6, 1666.

Milton's social nature is reinforced when we realize what a large part of his poetry is addressed to specific friends. I will take the liberty of quoting Parker's concise summary.

The fact that more than half of Milton's poems are addressed to definite people tells us something about his soul in relation to romantic stars that dwell apart. To read through these poems is to become aware of the author's associations with other human beings. He introduces us to his unusual father, a dearly beloved wife, his baby niece, and his boyhood sweetheart. He tells us of his affection for Diodati, Lawes, Young, Margaret Ley, Mrs. Thomason, Lawrence, Skinner, King, and old Hobson. We see him entertaining the Countess Dowager of Derby and the Earl of Bridgewater. We hear of his admiration for Leonora, Manso, Salzilli, Rouse, Fairfax, Cromwell, and Vane. For our benefit he praises the departed Shakespeare, Ridding,

102

# The Inner Life

Andrewes, Felton, Gostlin, and the Marchioness of Winchester. He makes us conscious of still other persons, unnamed, within and without his circle; convivial Cambridge undergraduates, hypocritical Presbyterians, Royalist officers, martyred Waldenses, a pious young lady, a wretched portraitist, an ignorant stall-reader. In sum, the Milton that we meet in the minor poems is a writer with a distinctly social tone. (p. 632)

One could go further than that. The majority of Milton's poems are not only addressed to friends, they are deeply person-oriented. Those poems are essentially about the actions and thoughts and feelings of or towards others. They tend to move from the limits of outer behavior into the inner limits of thoughts and feelings.

On the other hand, when Milton talks about mankind, or about masses or large groups of people, he displays a very different attitude from his feeling about friends or most individuals. I will review very briefly a few of his reflections on masses or groups of people. He had the same kind of contempt for the masses that was a commonplace in classical antiquity; Plato can stand as an example of the Greeks and Horace of the Romans. It continued among the Renaissance humanists. This attitude of contempt was widely shared among educated people of Milton's time.

In "Ad Patrem," his joining the company of learned men means, he says, that "I shall no longer mingle un-known with the dull rabble and my walk shall be far from the sight of profane eyes," and that prospect gives him delight. In the 1640s, his sense of superiority over the "common people" was strong. He has an amused sense of superiority in Sonnet XI ("A book was writ of late"), a contemptuous arrogance in Sonnet XII ("I did but prompt the age"—he having cast "Pearls to Hogs" and been enveloped by the "barbarous noise" of his respondents, "Owls and Cuckoos, Asses, Apes and Dogs"), and simple contempt ("To John Rouse," in which the Oxford Library is valued as a place

# John Milton

"where the insolent noise of the crowd never shall enter and the vulgar mob of readers shall forever be excluded"). Sometimes his description (in *An Apology against a Pamphlet*) of "the young Divines, and those in next aptitude to Divinity" who were (in Milton's view) "prostituting the shame of that ministery" by acting and overacting on the stage: "they thought themselves gallant men, and I thought them fools, they made sport, and I laught, they mispronounc't and I mislik't, and to make up the *atticisme*, they were out, and I hist" (*Prose*, I, 887). In *Eikonoklastes*, Milton was altogether scornful of the common people, calling them "an inconstant, irrational, and image-doting rabble," "the mad multitude," and "the silly people."

Milton made clear his distinction about the different kinds of audiences in his address to Parliament prefacing the *Doctrine and Discipline of Divorce*. He writes:

> I seek not to seduce the simple and illiterat; my errand is to find out the choisest and the learnedest, who have this high gift of wisdom to answer solidly, or to be convinc't. I crave it from the piety, the learning and the prudence which is hous'd in this place. (*Prose*, II, 233)

This is an explicit statement of Milton's usual posture in controversy. He had no interest in addressing "the simple and illiterat." He wanted to speak only to "the choisest and the learnedest," and to them he offered a challenge to mortal combat by words. "I crave it" is the knight's call for a boon before the combat begins. This was Milton's usual posture in dispute: he wanted single combat with an opposing champion of the highest merit. Milton was irritated when no one appeared, or when he was answered by a little man not worth his attention, or by an anonymous or pseudonymous character. The Black Knight appeared only one time: when Salmasius answered, Milton was in his glory; and he squeezed all the satisfaction he could out of the combat, which turned out to be rather a fiasco. It may have been this eagerness for combat with a known adversary that made Mil-

# The Inner Life

ton refuse to recognize it when he got hold of the wrong man in Alexander More.

Milton not only shared the common contempt for the masses. He also had something like hostility toward common people. In the *Second Defence*, in speaking of his second divorce tract, he says, "One thing only could I wish, that I had not written it in the vernacular, for then I would not have met with vernacular readers, who are usually ignorant of their own good, and laugh at the misfortunes of others" (*Prose*, IV, 610). In the preface ("The Verse") to *Paradise Lost*, he alludes to "vulgar Readers" who may think the lack of rhyme to be a defect, and (as I have already mentioned) asks in the invocation to Book VII that Urania may "fit audience find, though few."

His hostility toward the general public probably contributed, along with his overreliance on rhetoric, to his failure as a controversialist in pamphleteering. The story of Milton's last-minute effort to try to prevent the Restoration of the King is one full of pity for a sturdy loser. Although virtually everyone else recognized what the inevitable decision was, Milton tried to stop the "epidemic madness" of the people from insisting on government by "a licentious and unbridl'd democratie," despite the fact that the majority wanted a return to kingship. Milton acted on the view frequently held by educated people of his time (and of ours too) that it is up to the wiser heads to take over "where main matters are in question" and to compel the masses to do what is good for them (*Prose*, VII, 463, 438, 415).

Although Milton felt contempt for the masses, he had a high sense of the value of man; in the *Tenure of Kings and Magistrates*, for example, he says that "no one who knows ought, can be so stupid to deny that all men naturally were borne free, being the image and resemblance of God himself, and were by privilege above all the creatures, born to command and not to obey," and he recognizes "a mutual bond of amity and brother-hood between man and man over all the World" (*Prose*, III, 198-99, 214). In the *Second Defence*, he could say: "Since I bear no grudge whatever nor har-

# John Milton

bor private quarrels against any man, nor does any man, so far as I know, bear any grudge against me, I endure with the greater equanimity all the curses that are uttered against me, all the insults that are hurled, so long as they are suffered for the sake of the state, not for myself" (*Prose*, IV, 596). Milton's sense of respect for man and for man's liberty was boundless.

## V

Milton's deepest self is given form in his poetry. It is, however, a task beyond human powers to sort out what in his poetry is playing the precise melody of his own inner life, and what has been altered by the claims of convention and drama. Yet one can notice that some actions in his poems are in the same key with which we have become familiar from observing the events and the attitudes of his everyday existence.

In the light of my review of Milton's sense of others, I would like to see whether we can gain any new insights into his dramatic poems. Or from them, reciprocally, any further clues about Milton's sense of others.

For this purpose, I will consider only *Comus, Paradise Lost, Paradise Regained*, and *Samson Agonistes*. I recognize that that modest "only" encompasses a significant part of the best English poetry, which I approach with admiration, not to explain but to give some account of the group dynamics within each of these four poems. For this purpose, it is desirable to try to set aside all of our other conceptions of the poems. It is worth observing the relations of the characters to one another, the tactics used in their relationships, and the outcome of their interaction. From such a review, perhaps one or two useful patterns will become more evident than they were before.[12]

12. The techniques that Milton uses—in establishing relationships, for example, or setting up confrontations—are of course quite different in each of these four poems. Milton is a respecter of genre, however much he twists and expands it to serve his purposes more effectively. Each of these poems is of a different genre, *Comus* a Renaissance masque, *Paradise Lost* a diffuse epic, *Paradise Regained* a brief epic, *Samson Agonistes* a neoclassical tragedy. Despite the differences in technique, the essential patterns are observable.

# The Inner Life

In *Comus*, all of the action is subordinate to its enveloping grace as entertainment, featuring music and dance and poetry and celebration, taking place in a world ruled by magic. The dramatic action puts two parties into conflict with one another in the form of a morality play. (The poem has, in this structural sense, many parallels with *The Tempest*.)

One party is the closely-knit family group of two brothers, a sister, and an attendant Spirit who stands in the role of a father to the children. (The real father could not in any event have been made to appear in the original presentation since he was the chief member of the audience, of course, and his known presence there strengthens the sense of family in the masque.) They are cordial and trusting toward one another, and there is a sense of genuine affection in the feelings they express for one another.

The other party consists of Comus and his "crew" or "rout of Monsters, headed like sundry sorts of wild Beasts, but otherwise like Men and Women." The monsters have no relation with Comus except to serve as his machinery. Comus is a loner in the pure sense of the word; he has no relations with any other creature, neither wife nor child nor friend. Yet the idea of family is reinforced even with him, in something like parodic form, through the repeated references to his family, with Circe as his mother and Bacchus his father.

The family, of brothers and sister, is in distress at the loss of one member, and their sole aim—a corporate, human purpose—is to recover the lost one without damage to her and to reunite the family. Comus's aim is to seduce the separated girl; this aim is simply a fulfillment of his role, which is mythic and abstract.

The essential action of the poem is a dispute between Comus and the Lady. Their dispute is an extended exercise in argumentation and debate, consisting of an introduction (244-330) and a debate proper (659-813).

The debate is a rhetorician's view of human relations. Comus himself tells us, before the Lady appears, how he plans to persuade her: by appearing in disguise as "some harmless Villager" and approaching her

107

# John Milton

under fair pretense of friendly ends
And well-plac't words of glozing courtesy,
Baited with reasons not unplausible. (160-62)

On first meeting, he flatters her outrageously (244-70) but she
rebuffs him:

Nay gentle Shepherd, ill is lost that praise
That is addrest to unattending Ears. (271-72)

He tries to insinuate himself into her confidence and turns to
outright lies. When she continues unmoved, he admits the
strength of her argument in an aside:

She fables not, I feel that I do fear
Her words set off by some superior power (800-01).

But, like Satan–and Comus is much like Satan, in many ways,
both as he appears in *Paradise Lost* and in *Paradise Regained*–Comus
tries once more with lies after he has failed. "I must dissemble,"
he says, "And try her yet more strongly" (805-06).

The Lady's part is relatively straightforward in the debate.
She simply refuses to be persuaded by Comus's blandishments,
even though he makes a most appealing case to her against virgin-
ity and in favor of enjoyment.

Comus is, by turns, learned, authoritarian, inventive, and
witty. At one point (706-55), he makes as good a proposal for
enjoyment as "To His Coy Mistress" does. His speeches are
smooth, melodious, and easy (as in 11. 666-89), while the Lady's
speeches are rough, irregular, and cacaphonous (as in 11. 690-
705). Comus is, in every way, a better rhetorician than the Lady,
in both his general strategy, his tactics of argument, his diction,
and his skill in the general management of language. But the
Lady wins anyway. And she wins because she has, in this devel-
oping morality play, "the Sun-clad power of Chastity" and her
rhetoric–otherwise very ordinary–is therefore endowed with

such a flame of sacred vehemence,
That dumb things would be mov'd to sympathize.
(795-96)

# The Inner Life

Than which rhetoric can do no more.

There is a total absence of any real relation between Comus and the Lady. All is rhetoric, all management instead of human contact, all formal efforts to persuade and not be persuaded.

At the same time, some glimmer of human relations shines through. There is the true concern, to which I have already referred, of the brothers for their sister. And there is her rudimentary, elitist view of other people as we perceive it through the cracks of her understandable self-concern. When she hears the noise of Comus and his rout, she deplores them even before she sees them because the noise seemed to her "the sound / Of Riot and ill-manag'd Merriment" such as of "loose, unletter'd Hinds" (171-72, 175). We notice that their being "unletter'd" is against them; ignorance or lack of learning is a disabling feature. Even though she is lost, the noble young lady wants nothing to do with such trash:

> I should be loth
> To meet the rudeness and swill'd insolence
> Of such late Wassailers. (177-79)

The general attitude of the poem, in fact, seems to be unfavorable toward people in a crowd. Comus's monsters—at least half way men and women, and therefore perhaps worthy of some concern—are looked down on as "his rabble" (in the stage direction after 1. 658), as well as "his crew" (in "The Persons") and "his rout" (stage direction after 1. 813).

In *Paradise Lost*, the sense of human relations can most easily be observed by beginning with an analysis of the character groupings. This simple procedure may seem inappropriately sociological, but I use it because it conveniently leads to a view of how the characters look on the other characters.

The action of *Paradise Lost* can be thought of as involving three groups of characters. First, God's group, consisting of God, his Son, and the numberless host of angels in all their ranks and orders. Second, Satan's group, consisting of Satan, the third of the angels that rebelled with him and fell, and his progeny Sin and

# John Milton

Death. Third, Adam's group, consisting of only Adam and Eve and their prospective progeny.

The first group has an omnipotent leader; an essential family structure of father, son, and subordinate members; an elaborately hierarchical organization like a Model Army; and relations dependent on love and obedience. It is headed by the father figure *par excellence*. The second group has an exceedingly powerful leader, who (despite his formal relations) is essentially a loner; a parody of family structure in the figures and relations of Satan, Sin, and Death; the apparent remnants of a hierarchical organization but actual intrinsic disorganization; and relations dependent on passions (of the desire for power, avarice, anger, envy, and the like). The third group has light leadership tending toward co-leadership; a basic family structure; organization based on mutual decision within authorized limits; and relations dependent on love before the fall but increasingly dependent on passions after the fall.

None of the groups are absolutely stable. There is not only instability within each group, but also potential division inside the leader of each group. The action of the poem centers on the attack by Satan's group on the stability of Adam's group, as a way of attacking (paying back) God by thwarting his will. The means available to Satan are force, eloquence, and lies. Force is always impressive and dramatic (as in the encounter with Death) but never successful in the poem. Eloquence is usually successful, as in rousing Beelzebub and then the other fallen angels, in manipulating the conference of fallen angels to achieve the decision he wanted, or in the encounter with Chaos and Night. For Satan, eloquence often mingles (or is coupled) with lies, and they are usually successful, as in persuading Sin to unlock the gates of Hell, or in tricking Uriel. Hypocrisy (or dissembling), we are told, always has a chance of deceiving us because we are incapable of spotting it:

> So spake the false dissembler unperceiv'd;
> For neither Man nor Angel can discern

110

# The Inner Life

Hypocrisy, the only evil that walks
Invisible, except to God alone. (III, 681-84)

Satan's successes are presented as the successes of a master rhetorician. By his eloquence—his power over language—he can arouse the fallen angels, control their debate, cause them to choose his course of action, and persuade Sin to release him from Hell. His greatest success is, of course, his conquest of Eve. His success depends on his eloquence and his lies, and his eloquence depends—even more here than elsewhere—on flattery. (It is interesting to notice that Satan's heaviest flattery is directed at the only female figures of the poem, Sin and Eve; to the others, the angels and Death, his eloquence has at most only a flavoring of flattery.)

His approach to Eve is through the simple flattery of praising her beauty and her merits in deserving a train of angels and unlimited power (IX, 533-612). (In design, the encounter is almost identical with Comus's approach to the Lady.) Eve, like the Lady, is ambivalent toward his flattery, at first tartly observing that "thy overpraising leaves in doubt / The virtue of that Fruit," but in the same breath asking where the tree is located. Satan puts on the appearance of zeal, love, and deep concern in order to achieve the maximum in eloquence.

As when of old some Orator renown'd
In *Athens* or free *Rome*, where Eloquence
Flourish'd, since mute, to some great cause addrest.
(IX, 670-72)

And he uses all the measures of rhetoric to achieve eloquence. In due course, Eve succumbs to Satan's eloquence. Then, after transferring her adoration from God to the tree, her first wish is to share the fruit with Adam: not out of love, which was the basis of their relationship and the one they share with God, but out of envy that he may have another mate if she dies. Thus she adopts the relations of passion which govern Satan's group, and she compounds the change by adding a lie when she explains her reasons to Adam.

111

# John Milton

No person is more eloquent than oneself in the presentation of an argument that one wants to believe. Adam, a little weak, requires no Satan. He easily persuades himself by his own eloquence as soon as he has transferred his basic loyalty from God to Eve. And the Fall is thus complete.

Among the consequences of the Fall, the whole sense of others has been changed for man. Before, it had been the relation of love, as for God's group. Afterward, it is fatally tainted with the relation of passion, as for Satan's group, with the self before others.

*Paradise Regained* is, in its central action, a stripped-down replay of the action of *Paradise Lost* with different combatants and a different conclusion. Satan and Christ are set in single combat; Satan is introduced as "the Adversary" (I, 33), and Satan calls Christ "my fatal enemy" and "my Adversary" (IV, 525, 527). Their parties occupy a supporting or background role. We are not, however, allowed to forget the family nature of God's group, the identity of the father and mother of Christ, and the relationship of love; neither are we allowed to forget that Satan's group is, on the other hand, ruled by "their great Dictator" on authoritarian lines under the governance of the passion of fear.

Satan is a loner by inclination, and his resort to the demonic council is at first perfunctory and later out of bafflement. Even Christ is represented as having some of the qualities of the loner: he is made to seem altogether comfortable in the isolation of the wilderness, because he has thoughts lodged in his breast "as well might recommend Such Solitude before choicest Society" (I, 301-02). (The picture of Christ as a solitary intellectual is probably more in keeping with Milton's own inclinations than with the central Christian tradition.)

The combat between Christ and Satan is the central action of the poem. This encounter is doubtless like what Milton hoped for all through his pamphleteering life—that he could, like Christ, engage an adversary worthy of his powers, use all of the resources of eloquence at his disposal, and conclude with *The Triumph of True Rhetoric and the Destruction of False Rhetoric*.

112

# The Inner Life

Satan comes to Christ in disguise, as Comus had come to the Lady, as Satan had come to Eve. Satan's first disguise, as "an aged man in Rural weeds, / Following, as seem'd, the quest of some stray Ewe" (I, 314-15) is similar to Comus' disguise as a "gentle Shepherd," while Christ's physical isolation in a wilderness is like the Lady's being lost in a wood. Christ has the great advantage over the Lady—and over all of us—of being able to see through disguises, and the tactic of disguise therefore gives Satan no advantage. Satan tries his other tactic, of flattery (as in I, 468-90), but it is not successful either. How could one be successful in flattering Christ? Indeed, what tactic soever would have any plausible chance of success?

Milton has Satan and Christ carry out the actions described in the Gospel According to St. Luke. But the weight of the combat actually hangs on words, on Satan's effort to persuade by eloquence. The heart of the action is a series of speeches; each series consists of an appeal by Satan and a prompt repudiation by Christ. Satan's speeches are plainer, briefer, more abstract, and more intellectual than those to Eve and those to the Lady. And each time, Satan not only fails, but acknowledges his failure. Until, at last,

> Perplex'd and troubl'd at his bad success
> The Tempter stood, nor had what to reply,
> Discover'd in his fraud, thrown from his hope,
> So oft, and the persuasive Rhetoric
> That sleek't his tongue, and won so much on *Eve*,
> So little here, nay lost. (IV, 1-6)

Rhetoric of all kinds, flattery, lies, guile—all fail. With them also fails the effort to control another by the exercise of and the appeal to the passions of anger, envy, and the rest.

One comment by Christ on his sense of others deserves to be noticed. In the course of refuting Satan's effort to inflame his desire for fame and glory, Christ goes on to put down the generality of human beings:

> And what the people but a herd confus'd,

113

# John Milton

A miscellaneous rabble, who extol
Things vulgar, and well weigh'd, scarce worth the
   praise?
They praise and they admire they know not what;
And know not whom, but as one leads the other;
And what delight to be by such extoll'd,
To live upon thir tongues and be thir talk,
Of whom to be disprais'd were no small praise?

(III, 49-56)

These sentiments of the anti-populist Christ are altogether consistent with one form of Milton's own thinking, at least on some occasions in the course of his life.

In *Samson Agonistes*, the action consists almost entirely of verbal encounters between individuals, two at a time, with the Chorus hovering in the background. The basic character structure is that of a fractured family: a son with a father who is embarrassed by him at the beginning of the poem and with a separated wife who has betrayed him. Through the major part of the poem, love is absent from their relations. Only the Chorus, friends of Samson, has human concern for Samson. And Samson has only a little human concern for anyone, including himself.

The encounter of Manoa and Samson is a meeting of dissatisfied father and resigned son. The father regrets that his prayer for a child was ever answered, and his wish to achieve Samson's release is occasioned by his sense of obligation as father. Samson admits his faults and is prepared to accept any consequences without struggle. Manoa speaks for the outside, Samson from the inside.

The encounter of Dalila and Samson is a meeting of wicked wife and determined husband. The debate is a series of highly-wrought arguments by Dalila, first of conjugal affection and then of religion, with implacable denial by Samson of each in turn. It seems impossible to know, in the course of the debate, how to assess the motives behind her arguments because their surfaces are impenetrable assertions of "conjugal affection" and "Love's law," and self-exculpations of "the jealousy of love" and "common female faults." Likewise, we cannot tell whether Samson is wise or foolish in his adamant denial—which seems cruel and inhumanely suspicious—nor whether he has won or lost. All becomes clear only when the Chorus tells us, after Dalila's departure:

> She's gone, a manifest Serpent by her sting
> Discover'd in the end, till now conceal'd. (997-98)

Samson's earlier comments on her—that she is a "bosom snake," "serpent," "sorceress"—are thus validated, as is his recognition of her "bait of honied words" and her "feign'd Religion, smooth hypocrisy." The point is that Samson, though blind, has the power to see through hypocrisy in the way that (as we have been told in *Paradise Lost*) God can see through hypocrisy.

The encounter with Harapha is a pseudo-combat of hero and ex-hero. It is carried on rhetorically, with boast against boast and threat against threat. It ends in a draw, as each one simply fulfills his role without any real contact. The encounters with the Messenger are the formal machinery for Samson to reveal the decision of his inner promptings, which lead to the catastrophe.

Up until the conclusion, Samson is represented as a loner: in the course of the poem he limits his relations with others to formality and argument, except with the Chorus. Since all of the principal characters wish to make contact with him for their own purposes, it may be as well that he persists in such resolution and independence; and we think of him with that special regard we have for those who have been amply punished and who have suffered deeply.

There are a few other hints in the poem about the sense of others. The Chorus consists of loyal friends who are supportive of Samson; when they part, Samson comes about as close as he ever does to expressing human regard:

> Brethren farewell, your company along
> I will not wish, lest it perhaps offend them
> To see me girt with Friends. (1413-15)

# John Milton

The Chorus speaks slightingly of people in a crowd, calling them

the common rout

> That wand'ring loose about
> Grow up and perish, as the summer fly
> Heads without name no more remember'd. (674-77)

Likewise Samson dislikes people on holiday, as then they are (he says) "Impetuous, insolent, unquenchable" (1422).

At the end of the poem, Manoa seems to change his attitude toward his son, and turn from self-centeredness to selflessness. He is willing to use up his "whole inheritance," "all my Patrimony," to gain deliverance for Samson, even to living "the poorest in my Tribe, than richest"; and the Chorus commends the reversal by which a parent in old age nurses his child instead of the other way around. But when Manoa hears of Samson's death, his first lamentation is not for his son but for the loss of the chance for personal enjoyment and self-gratification: that is, the loss, the frustration, of his own selfish hope to be the one to free his son (1570-77).

Throughout *Samson Agonistes*, the characters mostly fill the roles that the fable requires of them. Even so, because of the power of the language and the extremity of the situation, the catastrophe rouses pity and fear. The characters do not express much human affection for one another, but the poem rests on the value of the family and of affection.

*

Some of the patterns in these four dramatic poems are recurrent in ways that tell us something of the control that Milton chose to exercise over his material. Although his narratives imposed some severe limits on him, he had (presumably) enough freedom to portray the relations of the characters in ways other than the ones he chose and to create different effects by emphasizing features other than those he singled out.

The crucial actions of the poems depend heavily on a single pattern: the encounter of two characters. The action that takes

116

place in larger groups is usually a formality. The two characters who transact the essential business are in an adversary relationship with one another.

An aggressive character is always trying to get the better of a more passive one. The aggressive character is destructive or self-serving; the passive character is put in the position of trying to defend him or herself against attack. Human feelings do not obtrude into the transaction. The main mode of attack is argument, and the supervening control is that of rhetoric. Many forms of eloquence are used in order to persuade. The aggressive character usually employs flattery, and it is usually recognized as such by the passive character. The language of the aggressive character is usually smooth and polished, and he ordinarily uses guile or cunning and often outright lies. The passive one uses neither flattery, guile, cunning, nor lies; his or her language is plain, often blunt, without noticeable recourse to the figures of rhetoric.

The structure of the family is an important pattern which appears, with more or less prominence, in all of the poems. The inference is always that family relations are, or ought to be, strong and influential, and the father is always a powerful figure of authority. Friendship seems to exist mainly within the family, and to be largely absent from other relationships.

The aggressive character has traits of the loner, and he has little feeling for other people. In truth, there is relatively little friendship or human feeling exemplified in any of these poems, with the modest exceptions I have already spoken of. The basic relation of love is described with respect and underlies all of the poems, but it is made manifest mainly with Adam and Eve. It may be that the lacks in expressions of feeling, which perhaps strike us almost unconsciously as absence of humanity, account for the fact that these poems–among the very greatest in our entire literary heritage–are more admired than loved.

These patterns are consistent with Milton's own sense of the world that lies beyond family and friends. The high value that Milton set on rhetoric is an important clue both to his writing and to his sense of others. He had the lifelong conviction that human behavior could be controlled by rhetoric. The eloquence of rhetoric is evident wherever persuasion is called for in his poetry. "For Eloquence the Soul, Song charms the Sense" (*Paradise Lost*, II, 556). In his poetry, he could create the response that he wanted to achieve. But he could not always do so in his own life. Nor could he with his prose essays, which are mainly efforts to persuade, all the way from *Of Reformation* in 1641 to *Of True Religion* in 1673. The failures of his essays—and of some aspects of his life—may be attributed in part to the fact that rhetoric is incapable of doing everything that Milton thought it could do.

The great successes of Milton's life, on the other hand, were related to patterns of family and friendship. These are the patterns that constitute the deep undercurrent of his poems. It is because of this stable undercurrent that the adversary relations can create their dramatic effect.

# Chapter V
## The Sense of the Natural World

———————— ⊗⫖⩊⊗⫖⩊⊗⫖ ————————

I BELIEVE THAT most readers who get pleasure from Milton's poetry count, among their chiefest blessings, passages which
describe the natural world. Other kinds of passages give pleasure
as well, of course, and the more kinds the better. I don't mean to
limit this comment to popular or non-academic readers—of whom
I wish there were more than there are—but to all readers, including Milton specialists, those who are budding as well as those
who are already in flower. All of us, I imagine, make some passages our favorites for a multitude of reasons that define our personal needs. Just as Milton wrote what he did, in the way he did,
in part to fulfill his own personal needs.

I believe that the lists of favorites of most readers would
include, prominently, passages about the natural world. Such as
lines from "L'Allegro," with Zephyr and Aurora a-maying

> on Beds of Violets blue
> And fresh-blown Roses washt in dew.

Or the picture of

> many a youth, and many a maid,
> Dancing in the Checker'd shade.

Or, for a second kind of example, the flower passage in
"Lycidas," with the congregation of

> the rathe Primrose that forsaken dies,
> The tufted Crow-toe, and pale Jessamine,

119

# John Milton

> The white Pink, and the Pansy freakt with jet,
> The glowing Violet.

Along with all the other flowers that are summoned to appear in order to be strewn on Lycidas's hearse and thus glorify it.

Or, for a third example, Eve in the Garden of Eden in *Paradise Lost*, with her gardening tools, when she first comes into Satan's view

> Veil'd in a Cloud of Fragrance, where she stood,
> Half spi'd, so thick the Roses bushing round
> About her glow'd.

She stoops to support

> Each Flow'r of slender stalk, whose head though gay
> Carnation, Purple, Azure, or speckt with Gold,
> Hung drooping unsustain'd, them she upstays
> Gently with Myrtle band.

I will not try to account for why we like these or similar passages. I would, instead, like to try to understand what lay behind them in Milton's thinking or feeling. How important was the natural world to Milton? What was there about it that appealed to him? In what ways did he view it? What did it mean to him? And what can we learn about Milton's inner life from such an inquiry?

I will devote a section of this chapter to each of the three poems to which I have already alluded. In each of these sections, I will take up some of the general questions that that poem raises about Milton's sense of the natural world.

## I

A clean, refreshing, outdoor spirit pervades "L'Allegro" as it trips along in its bouncing couplets. It is true that, in the course of the day and evening which make up the cycle of the poem, we get indoor glimpses of a cottage dinner and of a goblin sleeping on the hearth after his superhuman threshing efforts, the sense of a throng of city Knights and Barons, and of going to a play. But

# The Inner Life

mainly the scenes are outdoors, in seasons from the lushness of spring to the fecundity of autumn.

A good-morning greeting is given from outside a window

> Through the Sweet-Briar, or the Vine,
> Or the twisted Eglantine.

The landscape consists mainly of such scenes as of

> Meadows trim with Daisies pied,
> Shallow Brooks, and Rivers wide.

As soon as the maid can finish serving the dinner, outdoors she runs:

> And then in haste her Bow'r she leaves,
> With *Thestylis* to bind the Sheaves;
> Or if the earlier season lead
> To the tann'd Haycock in the Mead.

In fact, everyone seems eager to get outdoors, guided by the sun-loving impulses so strongly evident in well-adjusted English people:

> And young and old come forth to play
> On a Sunshine Holiday.

(The country dancers in *Comus* show a similar spirit, and have to be discouraged in the last song with the adjuration of

> Back Shepherds, back, enough your play,
> Till next Sun-shine holiday.)

The sense of the outdoors can be everywhere. Even Orpheus himself will be roused from his golden slumber on a bed "Of heapt *Elysian* flow'rs."

John Aubrey tells us that Milton "always had a garden where he lived." Not quite, but it can at least be said that when Milton chose a residence, he almost always chose a house with a garden— not an easy thing to do in London at that time, or since. That commodious house he took soon after returning from his continental travels was actually located in a garden, on Aldersgate Street; the High Holborn house opened on Lincoln's Inn fields;

121

the Petty France dwelling included a garden in the rear with a gate that opened into St. James's Park; and his last residence, the Artillery Walk house at Bunhill Fields, had a big garden and access to the exercising grounds of the London Artillery Company. Earlier, at Christ's College, there was an extensive garden, a pond, a bowling green, and shady walks; and the family houses at Hammersmith and Horton were in what was then the country. Aubrey recorded that Milton, after the midday meal, "used to walk 3 to 4 hours at a time," and he added that "his exercise was chiefly walking." (There could hardly have been time for much else.)

Milton had not always availed himself of the charms of the natural world. Both of the two extant letters from Diodati to Milton touch on the delights of being outdoors, and in one of them Diodati chides Milton for sticking too closely to his books and for despising "the gifts of nature." It is a passage full of affection for nature and for Milton, and it deserves to be re-read in this context:

> For what is lacking when the days are long, the countryside most lovely with flowers, and waving and teeming with leaves, on every branch a nightingale or goldfinch, or some other little bird singing and warbling in rivalry? Where are walks of utmost variety....But you, extraordinary man, why do you despise the gifts of nature? Why such inexcusable perseverance, bending over books and studies day and night? Live, laugh, enjoy your youth and the hours, and stop reading the serious, the light, and the indolent works of ancient wise men, wearing yourself out the while. (*Prose*, I, 337)[1]

It is interesting to notice how Diodati associates the gifts of

---

1. Diodati, in his other letter to Milton, prophesies "fair weather and calm" and "sunshine and enjoyment" for an outdoor holiday that had been postponed because of stormy days. "For tomorrow all will be fair," he writes; "the air and the sun and the river, and trees and little birds and earth and men will laugh and dance with us as we make holiday" (*Prose*, I, 336).

# The Inner Life

nature with enjoyment and with youth. Milton responded to the complaint against him (either this very one, or another like it in a letter now lost) in a verse letter to Diodati which we call Elegy I. He denies that he is always an indoors person or that he despises the gifts of nature. He said:

> But I am not always hiding indoors nor even in the city, and the spring does not pass without some profit to me. I also am a visitor in the grove where the elms stand close together and in the magnificent shade of a place just beyond the city's confines. (47-50)

This response bespeaks gravity and carefulness, in comparison with Diodati's ebullience and abandon. The answer is a fair one, however, and the elm trees serve well as nature's representatives. But there is little spirit to it, and no sense of affection. We know from Milton's other comments that his studies came first with him, by far, when he was a youth. Diodati's influence on Milton and Milton's confidence in Diodati were very great, however, and I suspect that this remonstrance made Milton rethink the value he put on nature. Later, as we shall see, Milton seems to have adopted, truly and deeply, the selfsame sense of nature that had belonged to Diodati.

All along, however, descriptive details from the natural world have their place, again and again, in Milton's poetry. They recur so often, in fact, that they create the sense of a familiar theme running through his poems.

Flowers have a particular prominence. Milton uses the comparison of infant and flower in "On the Death of a Fair Infant Dying of a Cough" to get his poem underway:

> O fairest flower no sooner blown but blasted,
> Soft silken Primrose fading timelessly,
> Summer's chief honor if thou hadst outlasted
> Bleak winter's force that made thy blossom dry.

The "Song: On May Morning" gives us a picture of

> The Flow'ry *May*, who from her green lap throws

# John Milton

The yellow Cowslip, and the pale Primrose.

In "Arcades" the Genius of the Wood calls the Nymphs "the breathing Roses of the Wood." Milton remembers, in "Epitaphium Damonis," the time "when I lay beside cool, murmuring Arno, where the soft grass grows by the poplar grove, and I could pluck the violets and the myrtle shoots" (11. 129-31). When Eve tells Adam about overhearing Raphael's warning, it was, she said,

> As in a shady nook I stood behind,
> Just then return'd at shut of Ev'ning Flow'rs.
>
> (IX. 277-78)

Not when the sun went down, or upon finishing work, but "at shut of Ev'ning Flow'rs." When Dalila first appears in *Samson Agonistes*, the Chorus describes her as standing

> with head declin'd
> Like a fair flower surcharg'd with dew. (727-28)

The flower world is thus forced into contributing to her dissimulation.

Milton gives his best attention to descriptions of the natural world, no matter who the speaker is and no matter what the occasion. For a single (and final) example, Comus's first encounter with the Lady brings out a characteristically rich description of where he had seen her brothers:

> I saw them under a green mantling vine
> That crawls along the side of yon small hill,
> Plucking ripe clusters from the tender shoots. (294-96)

Could he possibly find his way, at night, back to where they were seen?

> I know each lane and every alley green,
> Dingle or bushy dell of this wild Wood,
> And every bosky bourn from side to side. (311-13)

With such knowledge, the world is made real for us.

*

# The Inner Life

"L'Allegro" is an outdoor poem, yes, and descriptive bits throughout Milton's poetry recreate some reassuring sense of the natural world. Not a single one of Milton's poems with a specific setting is, in fact, an indoor poem. Every one of his poems that have specific settings—those with a strong dramatic element, *Comus, Paradise Lost, Paradise Regained, Samson Agonistes*—is an outdoor poem. All of them are set exclusively (or almost exclusively) in the natural world, or in its heavenly, hellish, or chaotic equivalent. A wood, a garden, a desert, a bank: these are the typical places where the crucial actions take place in these four poems. And many of the other poems—such as "On the Morning of Christ's Nativity," "Arcades," and "Lycidas"—depend heavily on description of features of the natural world for their setting, their development, and their effect.

It is true, I believe, that in all of these poems Milton is observing some of the conventions of the pastoral tradition, in some a lot, in some a little. The poems are peopled by a profusion of shepherds with their lambs, comfortably located in idyllic landscape. Milton's love of Virgil's *Eclogues* (along with his other favorites in that tradition) eases but certainly does not dictate his choice of settings, nor any other feature of his poetry. He never wrote a "pure" pastoral—nor a "pure" anything else: he shaped every tradition to his own needs—and his repeated use of the natural world as a congenial setting is, finally, his own choice.

In "L'Allegro," it is instructive to notice that, at the very beginning of the poem, Milton banished "loathed Melancholy" to an inside place (a "*Stygian* cave," "some uncouth cell"), in darkness ("where brooding darkness spreads her jealous wings"), and in a desert ("dark *Cimmerian* desert").[2]

This passage implies three oppositions: the *inside* (or closed place) as opposed to the *outside* (or open place), *darkness* as opposed

2. There are echoes back and forth between the "Cimmerian desert" of "L'Allegro" and the abominable man in the First Prolusion who should spend "a long and loathsome life imprisoned in Cimmerian darkness" (*Prose*, I, 232), and "those men who are born and lead their lives in Cimmerian darkness" of "On the Fifth of November" (1. 60).

# John Milton

to *light*, and *desert* (or lifeless place) as opposed to *garden* (or growing place). These oppositions are basic features not simply of "L'Allegro" but of Milton's poetry in general. They are of very great importance as a recurrent source of the fabric of his poems, but I can here only suggest their relevance to Milton's sense of the natural world.

These figures are often associated with one another. *Inside* and *darkness* and *desert* go together—at least two of them at a time—and the same is true for *outside* and *light* and *garden*. In each of these chains of association, the opposite figure is often alluded to.

The inside-darkness-desert set is often figured by dungeons, prisons, caves, dens, and caverns. They are all featured as enclosed, inside spaces, and they are usually described as loathsome, opprobrious, grim, horrid, constraining. They are generally associated with darkness and death. I will mention only a few typical examples, which can readily be multiplied by reference to a concordance or to the index of the Columbia Milton.

"On the Fifth of November" is an example of a youthful poem that is built on the association of inside-dark-desert. The foe, on "pitch-black wings," is likened to a tigress pursuing her prey through "trackless deserts at night in the moonless darkness," envious of the "fields rich in the gifts of Ceres." This "dark lord of shadows, the ruler of the speechless dead," puts on a disguise—the similarities to Comus and Satan are marked—and appears like one who wandered "in the expanse of the desert, alone among the hideous haunts of wild beasts." He flees at last to "a place wrapped eternally in the darkness of night," which is "the den" of Murder, Treason, and their fellows. Murder and Treason themselves live in "the inmost depths of the cavern," "a horrid cave" which is "dark with deathly shadows."

Comus is also a figure of darkness, and he naturally dislikes day. The sun is a "blabbing Eastern scout" to him, and he fears lest the "telltale Sun descry / Our conceal'd Solemnity." He demonstrates his distorted values by saying " 'Tis only daylight that makes Sin." The Lady, on the other hand, has her values Milton-straight in calling darkness "thievish Night" and "envious dark-

126

# The Inner Life

ness." The associations that come to her mind in darkness are within the darkness-desert sequence and are Milton's regular figures of foreboding:

> A thousand fantasies
> Begin to throng into my memory,
> Of calling shapes and beck'ning shadows dire,
> And airy tongues that syllable men's names
> On Sands and Shores and desert Wildernesses. (205-09)

In *Paradise Lost*, the first view that Satan has of Hell is of "a Dungeon horrible" with "No light, but rather darkness visible"; it is a "Prison ordained / In utter darkness" and "far remov'd from God and light of Heav'n" (I, 61-73). "*Chaos* and *ancient Night*" are, to Satan, a "darksome Desert" (II, 970-73), and Satan is "the Prince of Darkness" (X, 383). *Paradise Regained* has even more emphasis on wild and pathless desert and wilderness, with the same dark trip "from Hell's deep-vaulted Den to dwell in light" (I, 116).

In *Samson Agonistes*, the impact of the association of the inside (prison, dungeon), darkness, and death is multiplied by Samson's blindness. The figures of which I have been speaking all work together, with powerful effect, in Samson's lamentation:

> The Sun to me is dark
> And silent as the Moon,
> When she deserts the night,
> Hid in her vacant interlunar cave.
> Since light so necessary is to life,
> And almost life itself, if it be true
> The light is in the Soul,
> She all in every part. (86-93)

The sequence of darkness and cave brings us perilously close to death. Which is just where Samson is—perilously close to death. The Chorus's further lamentation reiterates the same figures, and through them the soul itself is brought into hazard—which is indeed the case:

# John Milton

Thou art become (O worst imprisonment!)
The Dungeon of thyself; thy Soul...
Imprison'd now indeed,
In real darkness of the body dwells,
Shut up from outward light
To incorporate with gloomy night. (156-61)

This is the most dangerous hazard that a human being can be put in. The soul, that divine particle of God's breathing, is in the darkness of despair.

The metaphor of the dark, enclosed space turns up in both expected and unexpected places in Milton's writings. It figures what is undesirable, and it sets up the open and expanding situation as the desirable one. In the Seventh Prolusion, for example, when Milton is arguing that learning brings more blessings to men than ignorance, he has recourse to this metaphor:

> When universal learning has once completed its cycle, the spirit of man, no longer confined within this dark prison-house, will reach out far and wide, till it fills the whole world and the space far beyond with the expansion of its divine greatness. (*Prose*, I, 296)

\*

There is another side, as there is almost always another side in Milton. The sequence of outside-light-garden is even more important in Milton's writings. The prominence of these figures is more obvious through the counterposed appearance of the contrasting figures of which I have been speaking.

The figure of light is undoubtedly the most pervasive figure in the entire body of Milton's writings. It is, moreover, supported by its associations within its sequence and emphasized by the figures of the opposing sequence.

Light appears from the beginning to the end of Milton's writings. It is in the Prolusions (particularly the First, of course, and the Seventh), in many of the minor poems, in the pamphlets (from *Of Reformation* to *The Ready and Easy Way*), in his letters

128

# The Inner Life

(such as the one to Philaras), and in all of his major poems. The figure of light has tremendous additional power in Milton's writings because of its acknowledged centrality in the setting forth of Christian doctrine, from the time of the four Gospels onward.[3] Still, it is necessary to be content, for the present purpose, with only a couple of examples.

Milton's central view of the values associated with light and dark are compactly set forth in *Comus* by the Elder Brother, that preternaturally wise youth:

> He that has light within his own clear breast
> May sit i' th' center, and enjoy bright day,
> But he that hides a dark soul and foul thoughts
> Benighted walks under the midday Sun;
> Himself is his own dungeon. (381-85)

But the *locus classicus* of the essential meaning of light in Milton's poetry is, of course, the invocation to Book Three of *Paradise Lost*:

> Hail holy Light, offspring of Heav'n first-born,
> Or of th' Eternal Coeternal beam
> May I express thee unblam'd? since God is Light,
> And never but in unapproached Light
> Dwelt from Eternity, dwelt then in thee,
> Bright effluence of bright essence increate.

All of the other meanings of light in Milton radiate from this central concept of God as light.

---

3. For one essential example, this passage from John 3. 19-21, the Gospel for Monday in Whitsun week: "And this is the condemnation, that light is come into the world, and men loved darkness rather than light, because their deeds were evil. / For every one that doeth evil hateth the light, neither cometh to the light, lest his deeds should be reproved. / But he that doeth truth cometh to the light, that his deeds may be made manifest, that they are wrought in God." The first collect for Whitsunday included: "O God, who as at this time didst teach the hearts of thy faithful people, by sending to them the light of thy Holy Spirit"; and the second collect for Whitsunday petitioned that "by the indwelling of thy Holy Spirit, we may be enlightened."

# John Milton

For Milton, light is so closely associated with God (or Heaven) and virtue that it sometimes carries one of the others as a meaning that does not need to be specified. In "When I consider how my *light* is spent," the *light* is not simply *life* (or, even more literally, *eyesight*), but *the divine gift of life*, or *the gift of God*. In Sonnet IX, the "Lady that in the prime of earliest youth" who concerned herself "to fill thy odorous Lamp with deeds of *light*," those deeds are *growing virtues* with a tinge of divine eternity about them. Virtue generates light, as it does in *Comus:*

> Virtue could see to do what virtue would
> By her own radiant light, though Sun and Moon
> Were in the flat Sea sunk. (373-75)

I will come back in the next chapter to the opposition of light and darkness as one of Milton's main ways of giving reality to conflict and crisis. So far as Milton's sense of the natural world is concerned, light was a—perhaps the—crucial feature. Light fills the open spaces of the natural world and creates its beauty.

## II

In "Lycidas" the speaker is not only in a natural setting. He is also in touch and in tune with the natural world, and the relationship between man and sympathetic nature creates a good deal of the meaning of the poem.

He sings the poem "to th' Oaks and rills," producing an introspective monody. He externalizes his grief and his other inner thoughts, and he addresses himself to figures in the natural world. He begins in "the still morn," with an apology to the laurel and to the myrtle for plucking their berries before they are yet ripe, and he sings through the day. He finishes at sunset and moves on; but, at the conclusion, he still has the prospect of continuing to be in touch with the natural world.

> At last he rose and twitch't his Mantle blue:
> Tomorrow to fresh Woods, and Pastures new.

But still "woods" and "pastures."

130

# The Inner Life

The body of the poem is in large part an appeal to nature to respond sympathetically to the death of a man. The speaker (as a man) and nature are to join in the mourning. The "Sisters of the sacred well" are asked to begin, and shepherd, woods, and desert caves

> With wild Thyme and the gadding Vine o'ergrown,
> And all their echoes mourn.

So do fountains, streams, the river Cam ("reverend Sire"), and St. Peter. Dolphins are asked to take part and "waft the hapless youth." Lycidas will become "the Genius of the shore" and will look after "all that wander in that perilous flood," like the spirit in "Arcades," the "Genius of the Wood" that looks after beasts and flowers. The general lament of nature for Lycidas approaches the reaction to the plight of Orpheus, "Whom Universal nature did lament."

"L'Allegro" provides a glorious natural setting, though a rather supine one. In "Lycidas," there is an active relationship with the setting. The death of a man is likened to death in nature.

> As killing as the Canker to the Rose,
> Or Taint-worm to the weanling Herds that graze,
> Or Frost to Flowers, that their gay wardrobe wear,
> When first the White-thorn blows;
> Such, *Lycidas*, thy loss to Shepherd's ear.

And the great flower passage (11. 132-51) is not simply a descriptive list of flowers. These are the flowers bespoken of nature, the special flowers which the vales and the valleys are asked to produce for the mournful purpose. Not just any flowers will do, and some of them must have their natures changed to comport with this sad occasion:

> Bid *Amaranthus* all his beauty shed,
> And Daffadillies fill their cups with tears,
> To strew the Laureate Hearse where *Lycid* lies.

*

131

# John Milton

Milton often used descriptive details of the natural world to represent the source of special delight for man. In his earliest extant composition, the Theme on Early Rising (presumed to have been written at age fifteen or sixteen, while at St. Paul's School), virtually all of his positive arguments in favor of rising early have to do with enjoying the natural world:

> Would you feast your eyes? Behold the purple hue of the rising sun, the clear brisk sky, the green growth of the fields, the diversity of all the flowers. Would you give pleasure to your ears? Listen to the melodious harmony of the birds and the soft humming of the bees. Would you satisfy your sense of smell? You will never tire of the sweet odors flowing from the flowers. (*Prose*, I, 1037)

He argues, further, that it was the charm of nature that made light sleepers of the lovers Tithonus and Cephalus; even they, noted lovers that they were, "would leave their beds to visit the fields with their adornments and dress of variegated flowers" (*Prose*, I, 1038).[4]

A classic appreciation of nature in springtime—and one of the most justly famous statements in all of Milton—occurs in *Of Education*. His memorable words, admirably compact, are the kind of pleasant declamation that he and Diodati used in writing to one another:

> In those vernal seasons of the yeer, when the air is calm and pleasant, it were an injury and sullennesse against nature not to go out, and see her riches, and partake in her rejoycing with heaven and earth. (*Prose*, II, 412-13)

The underlying assumption is that the natural world naturally

---

4. In the Elegiac Verses on the other side of the paper, Milton uses yet more descriptive details to tell of the delights that await man in the natural world: "Now the wild rose is breathing its fragrant perfumes; now the scent of violets is sweet and the corn is flourishing. Look, the bounteous daughter of Zephyr is clothing the fields with new verdure and the turf is moist with dew like beads of glass" (Hughes, p. 6B). Although these are mostly commonplace descriptive details, Milton makes them his own by choosing them.

gives pleasure to people, even that nature is an active force with which man can become personally associated. It follows that one should seek this pleasure, especially under the favorable conditions of spring. I believe that many readers, in focussing their attention on the classic statement, overlook what has preceded and introduced it. That is, that here is "another opportunity of gaining experience to be won from pleasure it selfe." Diodati had urged the connection between nature and pleasure, and Milton seems to be carrying out that idea.[5] But Milton goes further: he sees this pleasure that derives from nature as contributing, in turn, to human experience.

One extension of this idea is endowing the things of nature with human qualities and human emotions. This form of anthropomorphism occurs as early as the First Prolusion, in which the big advantage of Day over Night is the chance to enjoy the world of nature. But it is a world that acts very much like a collection of human beings:

> The kids skip in the meadows, and beasts of every kind leap and gambol in delight. The sad heliotrope, who all night long has gazed toward the east, awaiting her beloved Sun, now smiles and beams at her lover's approach. The marigold too and rose, to add their share to the joy of all, open their petals and shed abroad their perfume, which they have kept for the Sun alone, and would not give to Night, shutting themselves up within their little leaves at fall of evening. And all the other flowers raise their heads, drooping and weighed down with dew, and offer themselves to the Sun, mutely begging him to kiss away the tear-drops which his absence brought. The Earth too decks herself in lovelier robes to honour the Sun's coming, and the clouds,

5. The passage which I quoted from *Of Education* continues with Milton's version of Diodati's exhortation to Milton not to devote himself so completely to his studies. After the praise of spring, Milton says: "I should not therefore be a perswader to them of studying much then, after two or three yeer that they have well laid their grounds, but to ride out in companies with prudent and staid guides, to all the quarters of the land" (*Prose*, II, 413).

> arrayed in garb of every hue, attend the rising god in festive train and long procession. (*Prose*, I, 228)

This is indeed a kindly, affectionate description. The sad heliotrope smiles and beams at the approach of her lover. The marigold and the rose offer their lover a gift of perfume, held back for him alone. The other flowers raise their drooping heads and mutely ask their lover to kiss away the tear drops that his absence brought.

Suppose Milton could have raised his own head to the world and mutely asked to have his tear drops kissed away? If he could have done so, someone would doubtless have stepped forward, sooner or later—there is someone for everyone. What then? What would his life have been like? What would he have been like? Different probably, though we don't know. But he couldn't do that. He felt a little hostile toward the world of the masses of men, and he couldn't run such a risk.

What could he do instead? As a poet, he could convert the personal risks into the risks of poetry. He could endow the figure of a flower with enough spontaneity and with enough lack of inhibition so that *it* could ask for a response of affection. And the flower could respond fully and freely with the affection that Milton—and everybody else—wants. Milton himself—and of course his readers—could share personally in the flower's response.

Another extension of the classic statement in *Of Education* is the importance of spring to Milton. "The spring does not pass without some profit to me," he writes in Elegy I, and Elegy V is, in its entirety, a joyous celebration of the coming of spring. Milton introduces the latter poem by catechistically asserting the return of his poetic powers:

> Am I deluded? Or are my powers of song returning? And is my inspiration with me again by grace of the spring? By the spring's grace it is with me and—who would guess such a thing?—it is already clamoring for employment.

The employment it finds in the poem is to give a sensual, erotic account—very "unmiltonic" to the casual reader—of the effect of

# The Inner Life

spring on the gods and goddesses, whose lusty exercise extends through all their degrees. The lustiness does not stop there, either, as the coming of spring seems to affect the whole world. "Thus the wanton earth breathes out her passion," Milton says, "and her thronging children follow hard after her example."

Milton's love of spring extends through much of his writing. He was doubtless following in the tracks of writers of classical antiquity and their Renaissance followers in his praise of spring. In the myth of the golden age (as chronicled by Ovid in the *Metamorphoses* and by others) the season was always spring, and it was always glorious. But Milton also made the praise his own through personal experience.

The most touching passage in Milton about the effect on man of the coming of spring is in the invocation to Book III of *Paradise Lost*. These notable lines, the words of the poet now blind, also raise another issue about what man gains from his relation with the natural world.

>                              Thus with the Year
> Seasons return, but not to me returns
> Day, or the sweet approach of Ev'n or Morn,
> Or sight of vernal bloom, or Summer's Rose,
> Or flocks, or herds, or human face divine;
> But cloud instead, and ever-during dark
> Surrounds me, from the cheerful ways of men
> Cut off, and for the Book of knowledge fair
> Presented with a Universal blanc
> Of Nature's works to me expung'd and ras'd,
> And wisdom at one entrance quite shut out. (III, 40-50)

The special longing that this passage expresses is for the various pleasures of vision and of nature. But the passage is also a lamentation for the loss of something else that Milton thinks man can gain from nature. In a word, wisdom.

Milton had long felt that the natural world provided the opportunity for great growth. In the Seventh Prolusion, he speaks of

135

# John Milton

what he gained in the preceding summer from his relations with the natural world.

> I can myself call to witness the woods and rivers and the beloved village elms, under whose shade I enjoyed in the summer just passed (if I may tell the secrets of goddesses) such sweet intercourse with the Muses, as I still remember with delight. There I too, amid rural scenes and woodland solitudes, felt that I had enjoyed a season of growth in a life of seclusion. (*Prose*, I, 289)

The sense of seclusion is strong in Milton's concept of the natural world. In such a situation, in the privacy of nature–in an open, not a closed location–there is much to be enjoyed and much to be gained in growth and wisdom.

Milton may have been a little hesitant in his relations with other people. But the "certain reserv'dnesse of naturall disposition" that he attributed to himself did not quite apply to his feelings toward the natural world. His sense of the world of nature lacks the gaiety and the abandon that Diodati expressed, it is true. Milton's feelings are, however, open, sincere, and warmhearted. He made up for his reserve toward the world of man with his openness toward the world of nature. He had a rich and satisfying reward from that world.

## III

Satan begins his search for Adam and Eve at dawn in the Garden of Eden, hoping to find Eve alone. He hides "among sweet Flow'rs and Shades"; he seeks them "in Bow'r and Field," in "Grove or Garden-Plot," and "by Fountain or by shady Rivulet."

He finds Eve, at last, in a rose garden, tending the flowers. She is a figure in a landscape, only half visible among the rose bushes, "veil'd in a Cloud of Fragrance" of the roses. He goes toward her, through a stand of "Cedar, Pine, or Palm," "among thick-wov'n Arborets and Flow'rs," and she flows in and out of his line of vision as he walks along.

To Satan, the garden is gorgeous in its beauty, and he is almost overcome by it: "Much hee the Place admir'd, the Person more." He walks "as one who long in populous City pent" had come into "pleasant Villages and Farms" with "the smell of Grain, or tedded Grass, or Kine." Every sight and sound is a delight. He looks at Eve again: she is not only a figure in a landscape, she is also an epitome of the garden:

> What pleasing seem'd, for her now pleases more,
> She most, and in her look sums all Delight. (IX, 408-54)

The vision of Eve in the Garden of Eden makes Satan forget his hatred. He has, instead, the momentary delight of being half in love with her, whom he thinks "fair, divinely fair, fit Love for Gods" (IX, 489). Only half in love, however, and only for a moment. During that moment: which way?...toward love? He checks his impulses in that direction. Not toward love! By an effort of will (and of self-directed rhetoric) he regains his "fierce hatred" and "all his thoughts of mischief."

The natural world plays an important part in this first encounter of Satan and Eve. Indeed, its role throughout the temptation and after the fall is crucial: the natural world is the participant that measures and reaffirms, in cosmic terms, the meaning of what is taking place in human terms.

At the time of creation, mankind had been given dominion

> Over Fish of the Sea, and Fowl of the Air,
> And every living thing that moves on the Earth.
> Wherever thus created.... (VII, 533-35)

Adam is called "Lord" of the birds and beasts, and the particular responsibility of Adam and Eve is

>                     still to dress
> This Garden, still to tend Plant, Herb, and Flow'r,
> Our pleasant task enjoin'd. (IX, 205-7)

The natural world reacts sympathetically to whatever Adam and Eve do, and it reinforces the harmony of the created world. When Adam and Eve are ready to spend their first night together, and Adam leads Eve "to the Nuptial Bow'r,"

# John Milton

> Gave sign of gratulation, and each Hill;
> Joyous the Birds; fresh Gales and gentle Airs
> Whisper'd it to the Woods, and from thir wings
> Flung Rose, flung Odors from the spicy Shrub,
> Disporting, till the amorous Bird of Night
> Sung Spousal, and bid haste the Ev'ning Star
> On his Hill top, to light the bridal Lamp. (VIII, 513-20)

On a later occasion, when Eve noticed that Adam was "ent'ring on studious thoughts abstruse," she withdrew to the garden to carry out her special care

> among her Fruits and Flow'rs,
> To visit how they prosper'd, bud and bloom,
> Her Nursery; they at her coming sprung
> And toucht by her fair tendance gladlier grew.
> (VIII, 44-47)

The fruits and flowers not only profited physically from Eve's attention to them as a gardener, they also "gladlier grew."

The natural world reacts violently when they break the commandment and eat the forbidden fruit, and nature responds with something like horror. When Eve ate,

> Earth felt the wound, and Nature from her seat
> Sighing through all her Works gave signs of woe,
> That all was lost. (IX, 782-84)

And when Adam ate,

> Earth trembl'd from her entrails, as again
> In pangs, and Nature gave a second groan,
> Sky low'r'd, and muttering Thunder, some sad drops
> Wept at completing of the mortal Sin
> Original. (IX, 1000-04)

Eve's first act after eating the fruit is to worship the tree that yielded the fruit. "O Sovran, virtuous, precious of all Trees," she calls it, pledging it her care and her daily praise, and bowing low before it upon parting. What Adam and Eve had been given

138

dominion over now becomes, after her fall, the object of her veneration; the natural world thus becomes her god (IX, 795-838).

When Adam and Eve are inflamed by lust after the fall, they retire to a shady bank to make love.

> Flow'rs were the Couch,
> Pansies, and Violets, and Asphodel,
> And Hyacinth, Earth's freshest softest lap.(IX, 1039-41)

It is very beautiful, but somehow it is different from the way it was before the fall. There is now no vital relation between them and the flowers, and the flowery couch is simply a passive location in the natural world, like scenes we meet in "L'Allegro."

Afterwards Adam, seized by guilt, wants to hide in some dark, closed place away from the light, away from people, away from all relationships:

> O might I here
> In solitude live savage, in some glade
> Obscur'd, where highest Woods impenetrable
> To Star or Sun-light, spread thir umbrage broad,
> And brown as Evening: Cover me ye Pines,
> Ye Cedars, with innumerable boughs
> Hide me, where I may never see them more.(IX, 1084-90)

He addresses the pines and cedars in his time of need and asks for their help. They do not answer. They do not act. The relation has changed. Man is on his own.

But the human feeling still remains. When Eve learns that they must leave Paradise, her first lament is about having to be separated from the garden with its growing things. She yearns for what she has enjoyed and for what she has tended. In her thoughts, the garden comes before Adam:

> O unexpected stroke, worse than of Death!
> Must I thus leave thee Paradise? thus leave
> Thee Native Soil, these happy Walks and Shades,
> Fit haunt of Gods? where I had hope to spend,

Quiet though sad, the respite of that day
That must be mortal to us both. O flow'rs,
That never will in other Climate grow,
My early visitation, and my last
At Ev'n, which I bred up with tender hand
From the first op'ning bud, and gave ye Names,
Who now shall rear ye to the Sun, or rank
Your Tribes, and water from th' ambrosial Fount?
Thee lastly nuptial Bower, by mee adorn'd
With what to sight or smell was sweet; from thee
How shall I part, and whither wander down
Into a lower World, to this obscure
And wild, how shall we breathe in other Air
Less pure, accustom'd to immortal Fruits? (XI, 268-85)

Michael has to check her selfish and sentimental lamentation by reminding her that the garden hadn't belonged to her in the first place ("nor set thy heart, / Thus over-fond, on that which is not thine"), and that she does, after all, have the company of her husband, if not of these flowers.

*

These scenes in the Garden of Eden before and after the fall give some perspectives on the natural world which are different from the ones we have been paying attention to in connection with "L'Allegro" and "Lycidas." They represent the natural world as possessing–or perhaps having possessed, or being possessed by–mysterious knowledge and a power of action beyond the limits with which we are ordinarily familiar.

These perspectives, too, are part of Milton's idea of the natural world. They open up another sense of nature, and this sense is important to an understanding of how Milton felt about the world around him. He left us a good many suggestions, and some direct comments.

First for a general view of the whole earth, and all that is part of it. Satan is probably the first witness who was not prejudiced in its favor. After he has seen the earth, the sight of it fills him

with "inward grief" about what he has lost on account of his fall
from heaven. He longs for the delight that he could have simply
from walking around the earth, through the

> sweet interchange
> Of Hill and Valley, Rivers, Woods and Plains,
> Now Land, now Sea, and Shores with Forest crown'd.
>
> (IX, 115-18)

But he could find no joy from such a walk, he knows, "for only in
destroying I find ease" (IX, 129). Nevertheless, his passion
bursts forth in a loud lamentation. The pain is especially keen
because he recognizes that earth not only reminds him of heaven,
but it was built exactly on the plan of heaven, his original home,
and it may even be better than its model:

> O Earth, how like to Heav'n, if not preferr'd
> More justly, Seat worthier of Gods, as built
> With second thoughts, reforming what was old!
> For what God after better worse would build?
> Terrestrial Heav'n, danc't round by other Heav'ns
> That shine, yet bear thir bright officious Lamps,
> Light above Light, for thee alone, as seems,
> In thee concentring all thir precious beams
> Of sacred influence: As God in Heav'n
> Is Centre, yet extends to all, so thou
> Centring receiv'st from all those Orbs; in thee,
> Not in themselves, all thir known virtue appears
> Productive in Herb, Plant, and nobler birth
> Of Creatures animate with gradual life
> Of Growth, Sense, Reason, all summ'd up in Man.
>
> (IX, 99-113)

We can believe what he is saying in this painful soliloquy about
his first view of earth, as he is certainly not inclined to delude
himself. And we can believe that, in his view, earth before the fall
closely resembled heaven.

It resembles what Satan is impartially described as having seen
as he had sat, earlier, like a cormorant on the top of the Tree of

# John Milton

Life. From there was laid out before him

> Nature's whole wealth, yea more,
> A Heaven on Earth: for blissful Paradise
> Of God the Garden was. (IV, 207-09)

When Raphael made his trip to Eden to instruct Adam, he arrived

> through Groves of Myrrh,
> And flow'ring Odors, Cassia, Nard, and Balm;
> A Wilderness of sweets; for Nature here
> Wanton'd as in her prime, and play'd at will
> Her Virgin Fancies, pouring forth more sweet,
> Wild above Rule or Art, enormous bliss. (V, 292-97)

There might very well be some question about the validity of nature's wantoning and the orders that she gives out. Abdiel sternly lays it down—before he smashes Satan on the crest with a stroke that makes him recoil ten huge paces—that "God and Nature bid the same" (VI, 176).

God and nature may *bid* the same, but it is important that we do not attribute to Milton the view that God and nature *are* the same, or that God exists through his immanence in nature, or that the usual manifestation of God to us is the appearance of the Holy Spirit in the natural world.

Milton makes his distinction between God and nature clear in *Christian Doctrine.* He says that

> God's ordinary providence is that by which he maintains and preserves that constant and ordered system of causes which was established by him in the beginning.
>
> This is commonly and indeed too frequently called Nature; for nature cannot mean anything except the wonderful power and efficacy of the divine voice which went forth in the beginning, and which all things have obeyed ever since as a perpetual command. (*Prose*, VI, 340-41)

Milton is speaking strictly, as a theologian, when he defines nature as "the wonderful power and efficacy of the divine voice

142

which went forth in the beginning, and which all things have obeyed ever since as a perpetual command"–but not the divine voice itself. "No one, however, can form correct ideas about God," he says, "guided by nature or reason alone, without the word or message of God" (*Prose*, VI, 132). In answer to those who look to nature as God, Milton says: "There are some who prattle about nature or fate, as if they were to be identified with this supreme being. But nature or *natura* implies by its very name that it was *natam*, born" (*Prose*, VI, 130-31). This strict view of the relation of God and nature is also reflected in some of Milton's more informal comments, such as (in *Of Education*) that Hartlib had done so much toward reforming education under "the peculiar sway of nature, which also is Gods working" (*Prose*, II, 363). "On the Morning of Christ's Nativity" explains the winter weather by saying

> Nature in awe to him
> Had doff't her gaudy trim,
>   With her great Master so to sympathize.

All that is from the cosmic point of view. Milton also applies these matters to the human scale on which we all live. The existence of God should be evident to man, he says, because God has left "so many traces of his presence through the whole of nature, that no sane person can fail to realise that he exists" (*Prose*, VI, 130). Similarly, nature does its imprinting on us as well and gives us the guidance of "what we fetch from those unwritten lawes and Ideas which nature hath ingraven in us" (*Reason of Church-Government*, *Prose*, I, 764). These matters are further complicated by the relations of God and nature with conscience, reason, right reason, natural law, and moral law; but those questions are (fortunately) outside the scope of this essay.[6]

---

6. Anyway, here are a few clues; it is always interesting to notice the appositions that Milton slips in while he is in the act of defining. "No law can be *fundamental*, but that which is grounded on the light of nature or right reason, commonly call'd *moral law*" ("Brief Notes Upon a Late Sermon," *Prose*, VII, 479). "Further evidence for the existence of God is provided by the phenom-

# John Milton

The great human effort enjoined on man in *Of Education*—"to repair the ruins of our first parents by regaining to know God aright"—must be done, Milton admits, by the limited means at our disposal. "Our understanding cannot in this body found it selfe but on sensible things," he writes, "nor arrive so cleerly to the knowledge of God and things invisible, as by orderly conning over the visible and inferior creature" (*Of Education, Prose*, II, 366-69).

The search for learning, beginning with the conning over visible things, can lead us far into understanding the mysteries of the world around us. "What a thing it is to grasp the nature of the whole firmament," wrote Milton with youthful exhilaration in the Seventh Prolusion, "and of its stars." It would be a great triumph "to know the hidden virtues of plants and metals and understand the nature and the feelings, if that may be, of every living creature." But why are these things all here before us?

> The great Artificer of this mighty fabric established it for His own glory.... Do we perceive no purpose in the luxuriance of fruit and herb beyond the short-lived beauty of verdure? Of a truth, if we are so little able to appraise their value that we make no effort to go beyond the crass perceptions of the senses, we shall show ourselves not merely servile and abject, but ungracious and wicked before the goodness of God; for by our unresponsiveness and grudging spirit He is deprived of much of the glory which is His due, and of the reverence which His mighty power exacts. (*Prose*, I, 295-96, 291-92)

Still, there remains an element of mystery or uncertainty in the natural world. The Genius of the Wood in "Arcades" says that, in

---

enon of Conscience, or right reason. This cannot be altogether asleep, even in the most evil men" (*Christian Doctrine, Prose*, VI, 132). Christ tells Satan that good human productions are inspired by God, "Unless where moral virtue is express'd / By light of Nature, not in all quite lost" (*Paradise Regained*, IV, 351-52). God describes Satan's crowd as those "who reason for thir Law refuse, / Right reason for thir Law, and for thir King / *Messiah*, who by right of merit Reigns" (*Paradise Lost*, VI, 41-43).

# The Inner Life

addition to saving all his plants from nightly ill and to healing whatever the "cross dire-looking Planet smites," his music is

> To lull the daughters of *Necessity*,
> And keep unsteady Nature to her law. (70-71)

Similarly, the river in *Comus* needs a goddess, Sabrina fair, to unlock charms and spells with her precious liquors,

> Helping all urchin blasts, and ill-luck signs
> That the shrewd meddling Elf delights to make. (845-46)

These aberrations and their cure were minor, perhaps inscrutable, aspects of the will of God. Milton could have a special respect for the natural world in its entirety—and find joy and comfort in it—because it was carrying out the will of God.

## IV

Throughout his poetry, Milton recurs again and again to the portrayal of scenes from the natural world. They take their places with ease and naturalness, as if those places were their own, waiting for them. They create a sense of friendliness, of familiarity, sometimes even of affection.

Milton uses these scenes in a relatively straightforward way. Mostly they give a comfortable localization to what is going on, and endow it with the glow of reality. Often they have a metaphoric cast—such as the figures of light and dark—which enriches the action.

Milton's use of two special bodies of knowledge are really extensions of his use of the matter of the natural world, the vision of the world outside the self. I am thinking of his use—almost preoccupation it might be called—of proper names (for geographical places and for persons), and of his recurrent use of classical myth. From his reading, his head was filled with names (mostly of ancient or Biblical history) and with myths (mostly of classical antiquity).

The effects that Milton created with these two bodies of knowledge are often surpassingly wonderful. The music of some

of these passages is among the finest in Milton, who is probably
our greatest musical poet of the school of strong effects. Sometimes the passages are so splendid that a little intoxication seems
to set in and to keep him going beyond what is at least my op-
timum capacity. Even such a fine passage as the roll call of Satan's
principal associates (*Paradise Lost*, I, 338-521), with the geographical fixing and the history of the worship of each in ancient
times, begins to make my eyes a little glassy before the end is
reached. Some of the catalogs of people and places toward the
end of the poem (such as X, 671-706 and XI, 385-410) make me
wish for Michael's help in removing the film from my eyes, as he
did for Adam.

There is probably no way to be absolutely fair in citing passages of these kinds. Let me call attention, at least, to the fallen
angels, before Satan exhorts them to rise (I, 302-09), as they lie
there

> Thick as Autumnal Leaves that strow the Brooks
> In *Vallombrosa*....

A remarkable, memorable beginning, with the natural scene and
the place name supporting one another happily. But the passage
continues

> where th'*Etrurian* shades
> High overarch't imbow'r; or scatter'd sedge
> Afloat, when with fierce Winds *Orion* arm'd
> Hath vext the Red-Sea Coast, whose waves o'erthrew
> *Busiris* and his *Memphian* Chivalry,
> While with perfidious hatred they pursu'd
> The Sojourners of *Goshen*.

And so on. Here the natural world is overwhelmed by the names
of places and people and by historical accounts so compressed as
to seem unreal.

Or, for a final personal testimony, I enjoy letting my eyes wander, in "L'Allegro," with Milton's around the landscape

> Where perhaps some beauty lies,

# The Inner Life

The Cynosure of neighboring eyes.

I prefer that Cynosure to the one of the Elder Brother in *Comus* when he invokes the moon:

> And thou shalt be our star of *Arcady*
> Or *Tyrian* Cynosure.

These particular comparisons are perhaps unfair, I admit. But the fact seems to me to be that Milton almost always does wonderful things when his material is strong with details from the natural world. It is, indeed, hard to think of serious reservations to this proposition. On the other hand, when he is depending heavily on his reading of the kinds I have just been speaking of for the texture of his poetry, he is sometimes less effective. Occasionally he runs into sheer cataloging, occasionally into pedantry, occasionally into compression so complete as to lack vitality.

Milton's head was loaded with recollections from his reading, but his memory was also rich with details of the natural world. Some of them came from reading, but more of them seem to have come from observation and perception. The details are always sympathetically remembered, and sometimes remembered with affection.

He seems to have been comfortable in the natural world outside of himself. He took delight in nature and felt that he was better and wiser because of that relationship. He was not lonely when he was by himself in the outside world, and he had the feeling that the solitude of nature afforded him great opportunities for growth. Nature had a further special significance because it was, for him, a living testimony of the will of God. Though perhaps marred, as man was marred, it still displayed some signs of heaven. So it had an unusually deep meaning for Milton, who was always keenly aware of his own personal relation to God.

# Chapter VI
## The Sense of Crisis

---

MILTON DWELLS, most of all, on the crisis situation in human life. It is the moment of big decision that engages his interest. His concern is for those times when the individual is confronted by the gravest difficulties, the hardest tasks, the greatest risks, the largest opportunities for failure, the biggest chance to make the wrong decision, the threat of despair, and the easeful solution of giving up. His emphasis is less on striving for the glory of success than it is on gaining a triumph out of failure or coping successfully with a failure that is almost thrust upon the individual.

This description may sound like the tactics of a dramatist, especially the writer of tragedy. But Milton was not a dramatist in any regular sense of that term, and *Samson Agonistes* alone can be thought of (and thought of inadequately) as a tragedy.

What is at issue is, in fact, the reflection of Milton's deep view of the way the talented individual is obliged to make his way through life. Life is not quite a natural setting for tragedy, as Scaliger described the situation of tragedy in his *Poetics:* "All things wear a troubled look; there is a pervading sense of doom, there are exiles and deaths" (1561, Book I, chapter VI); but a little of that flavor is present in Milton.

The characteristic situation in Milton's writings is alienation. Villainy of one sort or another permeates all of the dramatic poems. All of the characters whose task is villainy are outsiders, unattached, unconnected, unrelated, without friends or family, at odds with the world. Sometimes other characters as well seem

# John Milton

at least separated from their world, as does Christ in *Paradise Regained* (perhaps for theological reasons, but perhaps not), as does Samson in *Samson Agonistes*.

I would like to discuss some of the ways in which the sense of crisis is central in Milton's writings. He brought to his task the unique sensibility of which I have tried to give the best account I know how to do: a complex sense of self, a particular sense of others, and a specialized sense of the natural world.

My account of what happens in Milton—and what I will discuss in this chapter—depends, first, on recognizing the confrontation of that sensibility with a series of crises in his own life. Next, on realizing the depth of the idea of conflict that runs through his writings. Further, on seeing how he perceived experience in terms of oppositions, and how he portrayed conflict through those oppositions. And, finally, on observing the key role that temptation plays in bringing conflict to the point of resolution.

I

In time of crisis, feelings struggle for control. Milton's own life was marked by a series of crises. To me, three are most obvious. One was interpersonal, one was physical, and one was political. All three were intensely personal, as every major crisis would have to be. All three doubtless had severe repercussions in the nooks and crannies of Milton's being, and in that sense were general psychological and emotional jolts in ways that we would find it impossible to specify.

The first, interpersonal, was the desertion of Milton by his young wife, Mary Powell. To review the bare facts.[1] They met in the summer of 1642, had a "courtship" of some form or another, and were married at the end of about a month's time. He was thirty-three, she seventeen. She moved into his house in London. After about a month of marriage, she returned to Oxford to visit

---

1. For a full account (including the facts, the fair inferences, the speculations, the rumors, and the wild surmises), see Parker, pp. 862-70.

her family. The "visit" was extended beyond what had been planned, and she did not come back to London in response to Milton's requests. The separation continued for a period of three years, and a reconciliation was at last effected through friends. Thereafter, they lived together continuously, had four children, and were separated only by her death (three days after the birth of their last child), in 1652, ten years after their marriage, seven years after their reconciliation, when she was twenty-seven and he forty-three.

I believe that Mary's desertion had a most profound effect on Milton, and that it was a shattering blow to his self-esteem. This is my belief, based on what I understand of the kind of man Milton was. This belief cannot be supported (or refuted, or modified) by words from the one reliable source, Milton himself, because no words escaped him about his feelings on this subject or on any aspect of it—or, if so, no record of them has ever been found. What he did write at this time, however, was voluminous: his four tracts in favor of divorce. The first was published about a year after Mary's departure, and the others within the two following years, all before her return. They are bold, strong assertions of the ideal of true marriage and the rightness of divorce under circumstances like his. I believe that they are his way of responding to her desertion of him: a sublimation of his feelings—anger, bitterness, regret, or whatever they were. But I doubt very much that this writing was enough to purge him of the deep hurt that he had suffered. That hurt would have to take another toll. Perhaps he is still working it off when he has Eve whine in response to Adam's severity after the fall and later propose the course of suicide, or when he presents Dalila as cunning and hypocritical in tempting the blind Samson.

I think that there was only one earlier crisis in Milton's life that came anywhere near shaking Milton as Mary's desertion did. It too was an interpersonal one: the death of Charles Diodati, his dearest companion, the one intimate friend of his entire life. There, too, he responded by writing about it in an indirect, sublimated way in the form of a Latin elegy. In that poem, the

# John Milton

conventions are dense but some sense of personal feeling is allowed to shine through. There, too, he waited a year—or, if some authorities are to be credited, almost two years—before expressing himself.[2]

The second crisis, physical, was his blindness. The first symptoms appeared about 1644, and his blindness was essentially total by late 1651, when he was not quite forty-three years old. It is hard to think of a physical disability more full of terror for a person who (like Milton) had devoted his days and nights to reading, whose learning had to be constantly extended to keep him in touch with intellectual currents, and who was deeply committed to the life of being a writer, especially a poet.

Milton frequently referred to his blindness, notably in the *Second Defence* (1654) (publicly) and in his letter to Leonard Philaras of the same year (privately). In a small way, Milton was a public figure, and his handicap was cited by opponents as a consequence of his wrongdoing. In his own references to his blindness, Milton's main point was always a denial that his blindness was God's punishment of him, or a claim that it was a natural calamity that had struck him.

Because of his blindness, Milton lost his efficacy in carrying on the work of his official position and was essentially supplanted. Privately, he could proceed with the basic tasks of reading and writing only with great inconvenience, and only with help from others.

He did express deep regret at his loss of vision, but he never voiced any passion at that loss. Of anger, for example, or lamentation about injustice, or whatever else at being subjected to this most disabling of all possible disabilities. He consoled himself,

2. The case of "Lycidas" should at least be mentioned. So far as I know, no one has ever maintained that the death of Edward King was a particular blow to Milton, or that it constituted a crisis in his life, or that he even had very strong personal feelings about King. But he wrote one of the world's great poems on the occasion of King's premature death. It is interesting to notice in the case of this pastoral elegy that Milton could set right to work on his poem and complete it within a few months of the death of King. King died in August 1637, and the version in the Trinity College Manuscript was dated November 1637.

# The Inner Life

more than once, with St. Paul's thought that "strength is made perfect in weakness." And, in 1652-53, a year or two after his blindness had become total, he returned to writing verse, after a poetic silence of some years.

We admire fortitude as a response to personal disaster, but the psychological price that the brave one has to pay is usually high. Milton's reaction to his blindness was truly remarkable, but I expect that it had an important effect on him in a way that he hid from the outside world and perhaps even from himself. But an effect that created a change in his emotional balance. Doubtless he purged himself of some part of his pent-up feelings by having Samson lament his blindness so vociferously and with such deep emotion.

The third crisis, political, was the Restoration of Charles II, the return to monarchy—and the repudiation of the principles to which Milton had devoted himself for more than a decade. Milton spent his full energy in a stubborn effort to prevent what was to him a cataclysmic disaster.

He did what he could. He wrote letters; he wrote ten proposals. In the very month before the Restoration, he published *The Readie & Easie Way to Establish a Free Commonwealth, and the Excellence thereof Compar'd with the inconveniences and dangers of readmitting kingship in this nation.* It is thought that he sent a copy to General Monk, and he later wrote a further argument in a letter to Monk. He then published a pamphlet against a Royalist sermon, and—in a last-ditch effort—revised and rewrote and republished *The Readie & Easy Way.*

All to no avail, of course, though at great personal risk to himself. He went into hiding after the Restoration, he lost much of his property, he was arrested and put in jail, and for a time it was touch and go as to whether his name would appear on the list of those to be executed. In the end, he was spared. Six months after the Restoration, the blind man was officially pardoned.[3]

The crisis did not end even then, however. He still had to sit by

3. Parker gives a superb, full account of all of these details in pp. 533-76.

helplessly while the world that he had helped to create was dismantled. In 1662, for example, universal censorship of the press was reestablished, and the Act of Uniformity was passed requiring all clergymen and teachers to accept the liturgy of the Church of England or be ejected from their places.

Milton did not write anything further on matters touching this crisis in his life, nor did he further reveal his feelings about it. Instead, he expressed himself once more in poetry. He went to work on *Paradise Lost* and completed his epic on the Fall of Man within the next five or six years.

I have focussed on these three crises because I think they were the most important ones in Milton's life. There may have been others that he felt to be of equal or greater importance. His rustication from Cambridge? The threat on his life in Italy? A vocational crisis in the 1630s about his decision to become a poet? A crisis in his Christian faith at about the same time? The death of his father, or of his only son, or of his first two wives? Who knows what else, of which no clue may have been left? Or where the clues are a little too obscure (as in *Lycidas*) to be sure that we know just what they signify? Whatever other crises there may have been, the pattern of those we know about seems clear enough to provide a basis for discussion.

Milton was more a man of words than he was a man of action. He faced personal crises without flinching. He seems to have worked off his feelings in words, usually indirectly, perhaps in ways that no one can recognize. But dealing with crises in this way ordinarily involves suppression. And suppression usually sets up emotional conflicts within the human being who deals with problems and crises in this way.

## II

Milton's writings are full of a sense of struggle. All of the dramatic poems are built around a fierce conflict between the characters. I described, in chapter IV, some features of conflict in discussing recurrent patterns of action. Let me add, here, a few

# The Inner Life

words about the pervasiveness of conflict in Milton's writings.

In these conflicts, one side (consisting either of a single character, or a leader with a group in the background, or several separate characters) is inventive, imaginative, and (above all else) aggressive. The drive to achieve is strong and unremitting, as if success depended mainly on tireless effort. Where there is a group, it has strong, driving, effective leadership. These qualities are similar to some of Milton's central drives.

This, however, is the side of villainy. But the motive for the villainy is not always clear. It is not quite the motiveless malignity that Coleridge thought he saw in Iago. It is more like the straightforward fulfillment of a role. The business of that role is to impose a struggle that threatens the physical or psychological welfare (or even survival) of the other party.

That other party is mostly passive and peaceable by initial choice, not eager to become involved in a conflict, but readily drawn into it as a matter of survival or principle. Its representatives are solidly virtuous, but they are not very engaging or interesting in whatever human dimension they are given.

Milton sometimes portrays conflict as action. When he does, he does it (as he does almost everything) wholeheartedly and even to extreme; and the results are stirring. The account of the war in heaven, in Book VI of *Paradise Lost*, is plainly the work of one who reveled in the story of a fight, and his rich inventiveness is a delight to the reader: Abdiel's noble stroke on Satan's proud crest that sends him reeling for ten huge paces, the overnight invention of devilish engines that throw the angels into disorder, the pulling up of mountains to crush the foe, and that final leap of horror and confusion into the empty void. The story consumes almost a tenth of the total length of the entire poem—far more than its importance to the plot of the poem would seem to warrant, but not more than the relish of its telling justifies. Likewise, the meeting of Satan, Sin, and Death (II, 629-844) is justly valued as the story of a physical encounter that becomes increasingly frightening as it proceeds. The terrorizing tactics of the two antagonists approach the very verge of combat that would pit the

155

irresistible against the impregnable–until the fight is averted at the last possible moment.

The most telling and impressive kind of action in Milton's dramatic poems, however, is verbal action. This action also represents struggle and implies conflict. All of the main speaking characters are well trained in the art of rhetoric, and most of their talk is an effort to persuade–either to persuade others, or to refute those who are trying to persuade them, or (in a few cases) to persuade themselves. Examples abound: Comus, Satan in both epics, and the three main visitors to Samson are the obvious persuaders of the aggressive cast. The first Council in Hell (*Paradise Lost*, I, 1-505) is the most celebrated (and justly celebrated) of dozens of examples in which speeches are used to carry on a struggle and bring it to a resolution. The characters face a lot of crises in Milton's poems, and they deal with those crises in a characteristic way–by giving speeches about them.

A word about the prose. Milton's essays are for the most part polemical in their nature, of course, and the sense of conflict is strong in them. Usually he argues that the present situation of the subject on which he is writing is seriously at fault and that it requires some action–preferably immediately–to remedy the problem. Often he associates this sense of immediacy, or critical need, with the situation at hand. From the tone that Milton usually adopted in his essays, and the frequency with which he adopted it, he seems to have had a love of controversy and an eagerness to take sides in a conflict.

## III

It may be that Milton's sense of conflict is most truly revealed within the texture of his language. I am thinking of his fondness for oppositions. Some of the most frequent ones, to which he returns again and again, are setting the inside in opposition to the outside, or the body in opposition to the spirit, or strength in opposition to weakness, or high (up) in opposition to low (down). Opposites and contraries abound, as does dialectical thinking, in

# The Inner Life

the prose and the poetry. "L'Allegro" and "Il Penseroso" can stand as a symbolic example of his use of opposition to further his purposes.

The most notable and frequent opposition in Milton, however, is light as opposed to darkness. This opposition runs throughout his works, from his undergraduate exercises through his last major poems. Let me offer a few hints about the sense of conflict that the opposition of light and darkness signifies.

I imagine that the first passage that comes to the minds of most of us in connection with the subject of light and darkness is the great apostrophe to light—"Hail holy Light, offspring of Heav'n first-born"—the invocation to Book III of *Paradise Lost*. It is a glorious passage, full of reverence and joy, in verse that echoes and re-echoes in the memory.

I am not sure, however, whether the depth of the opposition of light and darkness in this passage is not obscured by the harmonious numbers. The first twelve lines celebrate pure light, indeed; but the entire remainder of the invocation—the other forty-three lines—celebrate the poet's return from darkness into light, lament the darkness of his blindness, and rejoice at the celestial light that shines inward into that eyeless darkness.

Perhaps the other passage that most of us think of on the subject of light and darkness is part of Samson's very first speech. It is his heartfelt lamentation at his blindness. "Light the prime work of God to me is extinct," he says; "I dark in light expos'd" and "Scarce half I seem to live, dead more than half." Samson's life in darkness makes more poignant the loss of light. The light and the dark are tied together, but each is pulling in the opposite direction:

> O dark, dark, dark, amid the blaze of noon,
> Irrecoverably dark, total Eclipse
> Without all hope of day!
> O first created Beam, and thou great Word,
> "Let there be light, and light was over all";
> Why am I thus bereav'd thy prime decree?

157

# John Milton

In chapter V, I called attention to some of Milton's regular associations with darkness (inside-desert-death) and those with light (outside-garden-life). These associations are mostly all evident in this entire speech by Samson.

Samson's plight creates a deep emotional impact. It makes real, in this touching passage, the fundamental opposition of light and darkness:

> The Sun to me is dark
> And silent as the Moon,
> When she deserts the night,
> Hid in her vacant interlunar cave.
> Since light so necessary is to life,
> And almost life itself, if it be true
> That light is in the Soul,
> She all in every part; why was the sight
> To such a tender ball as th' eye confin'd?
> So obvious and so easy to be quench't,
> And not as feeling through all parts diffus'd,
> That she might look at will through every pore?
> Then had I not been thus exil'd from light;
> As in the land of darkness yet in light,
> To live a life half dead, a living death,
> And buried.

Here the words that are associated with light and dark make the opposition explicit and indicate the conflict between the two.

The idea of opposition is, in fact, a central theme through Milton's writings, and the idea is often figured by the opposition of light and darkness, or day and night. Let me mention a few examples which are perhaps less easily remembered than those in the great poems.

In *Reason of Church-Government*, Milton defends the existence of secrets and errors on the grounds that they are sent by God as "an incitement" to us. "For," he says, "if there were no opposition where were the triall of an unfained goodnesse and magnanimity? vertue that wavers is not vertue, but vice revolted from itselfe,

and after a while returning." We need this conflict, he argues. He
goes forward with this idea of the importance of opposition in the
next few sentences, which I will quote for the purpose of showing how much Milton relies on light and dark to carry the idea
out. On the one hand, "do not darken" "shining light" and
"perfet day" cluster together, and on the other hand stands "the
way of the wicked is as darknesse":

> The actions of just and pious men do not darken in their
> middle course; but *Solomon* tels us they are as the shining
> light, that shineth more and more unto the perfet day. But if
> we shall suffer the trifling doubts and jealousies of future
> sects to overcloud the faire beginnings of purpos't reforma-
> tion, let us rather fear that another proverb of the same
> Wiseman be not upraided to us, that the way of the wicked
> is as darknesse, they stumble at they know not what. (*Prose*,
> I, 795)

As early as the First Prolusion, Milton as an undergraduate
chose to make the simple alternation of day and night into a
struggle on the part of two personified abstractions, and to argue
that they have mutual repulsion and unremitting hatred for one
another. He ventured to chide the ancient writers for figuring day
as a suitor for the hand of night

> when their perpetual alternation and mutual repulsion, as it
> were, could be indicated far better by the figure of an innate
> and unremitting hatred? for it is well known that light and
> darkness have been divided from one another by an implaca-
> ble hatred from the very beginning of time. (*Prose*, I, 224-25)

Of course this undergraduate exercise contains a lot of bom-
bast. But his heart was in it. He introduces his ringing peroration
by asking that "by your leave I may add a few words which I
cannot well omit."

> With good reason, then [he begins], have the poets declared
> that Night springs from Hell, since by no means whatever
> could so many grievous ills descend upon mankind from any

other quarter. For when night falls all things grow foul and vile. (*Prose*, I, 230)

And so on with an amusing tirade in which night and death end up as bedfellows. It was a thought that stayed with him. In his touching letter to Leonard Philaras in 1654, he is still talking about the "many days of darkness" that is everyone's destiny but that "the signal kindness of Providence" had made his "more mild" than "lethal."

Often the opposition of light and dark is more subtle in Milton, but it is still evident if we take the trouble to notice the kinds of terms that stand for and are associated with light, and those that stand for and are associated with darkness. This passage from *Of Reformation* is, I think, a good and fair example:

> When I recall to mind at last, after so many darke Ages, wherein the huge overshadowing traine of *Error* had almost swept all the Starres out of the Firmament of the *Church*; how the bright and blissfull *Reformation* (by Divine Power) strook through the black and settled Night of *Ignorance* and *Antichristian Tyranny*, me thinks a soveraigne and reviving joy must needs rush into the bosome of him that reads or heares; and the sweet Odour of the returning *Gospell* imbath his Soule with the fragrancy of Heaven. (*Prose*, I, 524)

Typically, also, later in that same pamphlet Milton makes the opposition absolutely explicit: "The very essence of Truth is plainnesse, and brightnes; the darknes and crookednesse is our own" (*Prose*, I, 566).

Such passages recur again and again. They point to a characteristic in Milton which it is illuminating to recognize. That is his tendency to polarize qualities which are related but different, or to set up oppositions. He appears to have perceived a kind of pervading conflict working at the heart of human experience.

## V

In a world of conflict, choices abound. In Milton's view, many forces are at work to encourage or persuade us to make a choice that will turn out to have been reprehensible. The temptation to make a choice which is morally wrong is the controlling event in every one of Milton's major dramatic poems. The resolution of the central action of each of those poems depends entirely on the choice made in the face of temptation. More than that, the idea of temptation is–as I am sure most readers recognize–a central theme that runs throughout Milton's writings.

In the same way that Milton thought opposition was a necessary test of virtue, so he held as a settled principle that temptation was essential to our moral well being: "that which purifies us is triall, and triall is by what is contrary." The full passage from *Areopagitica* is the classic statement of one of Milton's central beliefs:

> As therefore the state of man now is; what wisdome can there be to choose, what continence to forbeare without the knowledge of evill? He that can apprehend and consider vice with all her baits and seeming pleasures, and yet abstain, and yet distinguish, and yet prefer that which is truly better, he is the true warfaring Christian. I cannot praise a fugitive and cloister'd vertue, unexercis'd & unbreath'd, that never sallies out and sees her adversary, but slinks out of the race, where that immortall garland is to be run for, not without dust and heat. Assuredly we bring not innocence into the world, we bring impurity much rather: that which purifies us is triall, and triall is by what is contrary. That vertue therefore which is but a youngling in the contemplation of evill, and knows not the utmost that vice promises to her followers, and rejects it, is but a blank vertue, not a pure. (*Prose*, II, 514-16)[4]

4. Milton discusses temptation at length in *Christian Doctrine*, Book I, chapter VIII, "Of the Providence of God, or of his Universal Government of Things." "Temptation is either good or evil. It is evil when God...either withdraws his grace from a man or throws opportunities for sin in his path or hardens his heart or blinds him.... Good temptations are those which God uses to tempt even righteous men, in order to prove them. He does this not for his own sake–as if he did not know what sort of men they would turn out to be–but either to

# John Milton

Milton certainly provides ample opportunity for his leading characters to be true warfaring (as well as wayfaring) Christians. They are made to sally out and meet their adversaries, not without dust and heat; they do not slink out of the race, and they are offered the baits and seeming pleasures of vice.

The main characters have a number of things in common when it is their lot to confront temptation. In the first place, each one is isolated from human companionship, and is without the succor of any outside advice or help. In Milton's scheme, there is nothing joint or corporate or shared about temptation. You are on your own, with whatever inner resources you possess, from whatever source: it is a lonely private act of the individual. You must succeed alone, or you will fail alone.

The temptations challenge the moral and spiritual welfare of the one tempted. The struggle is within; its progress is externalized by the accounts of speech. We can follow the evident stage of the temptation, almost as if it were a battle being fought on the field of the mind or spirit.

The tempter is always a skillful and experienced foe, always bright, clever, witty, and persuasive, always a little mysterious. In addition, the tempter uses disguises, dissembles and equivocates, tells outright lies, and often has special powers (of changing his appearance, for example) that seem magical. The tempter is generally given better poetry to speak than is the one being tempted. Often this is part of the rhetoric of temptation, but sometimes the finest passages are not even part of his baits and seeming pleasures, like Comus's first speech, "The Star that bids the Shepherd fold"–which is, I think, the gayest, smoothest, and most joyous passage in the whole poem. In all, the tempter appears to have many advantages over the one being tempted, who seems comparatively unsophisticated.

---

exercise or demonstrate their faith or patience.... Good temptation, then, is rather to be desired.... But even the faithful are sometimes insufficiently aware of all these methods of divine providence, until they examine the subject more deeply and become better informed about the word of God" (*Prose*, VI, 338-39).

# The Inner Life

More than that, the temptations are intrinsically attractive, with appeal to all of the senses. Milton thought enough of a passage by Tertullian (which he had read in a 1634 edition of the works of that worthy) to copy it off into his Commonplace Book. "No one combines poison with gall, and with hellebore," Tertullian had written, "but with savory sauces and delicacies.... So the devil steeps whatever deadly dish he prepares in God's dearest...benefits." In front of Tertullian's words, Milton placed his own comment: "In moral evil much good can be mixed and that with remarkable cunning" (*Prose*, I, 362). And he himself followed the devil's formula when he was preparing dishes for the devils to serve.

I would like to focus, very briefly, on the main temptation scene in each of the four dramatic poems. I have already given, in chapter IV, my idea of the group dynamics or interactions of the characters in these poems. I will try to supplement those remarks (which treat an important context for the temptations) by speaking here only of the essential act of temptation and what it means in the context of struggle, conflict, and crisis.

The crux of the entire action of *Comus* is the scene of temptation when Comus has the Lady seated in an enchanted chair, surrounded by dainties and enveloped with soft music. The temptation to give up her virtue (659-813) is symbolized by the appeal for her to drink from his cup. Her eyes are not deceived by the enchantments ("lickerish baits," she calls them), and her mind is not taken in by his arguments ("false rules prankt in reason's garb"). She is unshakeably resolute, and the temptations fails.

In *Paradise Lost*, the action reaches its climax with the temptation of Eve (IX, 533-794), symbolized by the appeal for her to eat the forbidden fruit. The complex temptation, in the garden of fragrant flowers, goes through several stages: flattery of her as a person (to which she is not immune), praise of the tree and the offer to show it to her (which intrigue her), arguments to counteract her first refusal (which attract her), and her decision to eat the fruit. She is irresolute, she is taken in by the arguments, and the temptation succeeds.

# John Milton

In *Paradise Regained*, the action of the whole poem is a series of temptations of Christ by Satan. The poem is a continued encounter of two adversaries who are engaged in an earth-shaking struggle with one another. Christ instantly repudiates every kind of appeal that Satan can offer: flattery, the sensual delight of a banquet, wealth, fame and glory, rule of the world, pride. Christ is absolutely resolute in the struggle. Satan, on the other hand, is irresolute, sometimes almost half-hearted in proferring his temptations, but stubborn enough to keep trying even though he seems to realize that he can't win. The temptations fail, of course, Satan is vanquished in the conflict, and Christ is hailed as the "Queller of Satan" and the "Victor."

In *Samson Agonistes*, temptation takes a different form. Each of the encounters that make up the body of the poem is a conflict which turns out to be a separate temptation. Manoa wants to persuade Samson to accept a deal which he is trying to arrange with the Philistines to get him released. Dalila wants to persuade him to come home with her if she can work it out with the Philistines. Harapha wants to inflate himself by making a favorable comparison with Samson. In fact, the temptation that each one holds in front of Samson is that of getting him to give up: meekly accepting Manoa's arrangement, thankfully leaving the "loathsome prison-house" to live with Dalila, or knuckling under to the plainly superior physical force of Harapha.

Samson does none of the things he is tempted to do. He does not give up, and he is absolutely resolute in maintaining his position. He triumphs over all of these temptations.

The last temptation is the demand by the Philistines, delivered by the Messenger, for him to give public proof of his strength at their feast. Samson wavers in his understanding of this demand–and the reasons for his wavering will be part of the subject for the next chapter, as will his earlier temptation–before he accepts. And it turns out that his acceptance is itself a final triumph over the temptation of improper self-assertion, as opposed to the acceptance of God's will.

164

# The Inner Life

It is interesting to notice how much the main temptations of all four of these poems have in common. Flattery is a regular pre-amble to the temptation. Delight in things that appeal to the senses (especially food, but also music and flowers) plays a big part in both setting up and symbolizing the temptation. Arguments (false but attractive) are supposed to try to effect persuasion. One other common matter: despair is often lurking around the corner, ready to test the fallen or dispirited, and despair is just about the ultimate temptation. Milton has special concern for this threat, particularly in *Paradise Lost* and *Samson Agonistes*, where there is most need for concern.

Of course other temptations are evident throughout Milton, and they form an important part of the basic texture of his writings. I will not, however, try to catalog them.

What is impressive to me is the fact that temptation seems to be the ultimate form of conflict in Milton. Conflict was, for him, a purifying form of experience, and opposition was the way he seems to have perceived the human mode of existence. It is only the one tempted who can finally profit from temptation; the tempter is an instrumental agent. Temptation makes possible the development of heroic patience under adversity. The trial of faith helps to shape both the character of the one tested and also the role that he or she is capable of filling. In this troubled world, it is temptation that brings crisis up to a state of resolution.

# Chapter VII
## The Sense of Guidance

---

SAMSON AGONISTES BEGINS on the emotional level at which *Paradise Lost* leaves off. Adam and Eve are ushered out of Paradise by the angel Michael, following the blazing sword of God. Beyond the gate, they look back and see a throng of dreadful faces, fiery arms, and the flaming brand high above the gate to what has always been their home. Always. From the beginning of human time.

They start to weep at their ejection from Paradise. But they have had a promise that they will possess "A paradise within thee, happier far." And they have also been promised that, in the future, God's faithful people will be guided and defended by the Spirit of God. They wipe away their tears, and they step forth into a new world:

> The World was all before them, where to choose
> Thir place of rest, and Providence thir guide:
> They hand in hand with wand'ring steps and slow,
> Through *Eden* took thir solitary way.

And so *Paradise Lost* concludes, with a sense of fellow feeling for Adam and Eve. Milton conveys compassion for them at having to suffer the consequences of their actions, respect for their firm reaction to the fearful prospect, pleasure in their display of confidence and faith, and hope that they can manage well in the world of choice before them. With Providence their guide.

Samson is being led by a "guiding hand" at the beginning of

167

# John Milton

*Samson Agonistes*. He has been released for the day from his chains in the dank prison. He is being guided to a bank with choice of sun or shade, in the pure and sweet air of heaven.

> A little onward lend thy guiding hand
> To these dark steps, a little further on;
> For yonder bank hath choice of Sun or shade,
> There I am wont to sit, when any chance
> Relieves me from my task of servile toil,
> Daily in the common Prison else enjoin'd me,
> Where I a Prisoner chain'd, scarce freely draw
> The air imprison'd also, close and damp,
> Unwholesome draught: but here I feel amends,
> The breath of Heav'n fresh-blowing, pure and sweet,
> With day-spring born; here leave me to respire.

Milton conveys a sense of compassion for Samson at the beginning of the poem, as he did for Adam and Eve at the end of *Paradise Lost*. Samson has already suffered grave consequences for his actions, and no end to his suffering is in sight. He has borne up under the punishment of having his eyes put out and the ignominy of being treated like an animal in the common prison house. We should recognize this sense of compassion as another of Milton's recurrent themes, reflecting yet one more feature of his nature.

Samson isn't left to respire for very long where the guiding hand has left him. Nearly everybody in the poem wants to guide him to do or to accept something or other. The Chorus wants to guide him out of dejection, out of taxing divine disposal. Manoa wants to guide him to accept the deal he is making with the Philistines to ransom him out of further punishment. Dalila wants to guide him to accept her once more and return to live with her. The Messenger is directed by the Philistine lords to guide him to the Assembly; as Samson leaves, the Chorus says, "Go, and the Holy One / Of *Israel* be thy guide" (1427-28). In the report of the catastrophe, we learn that Samson was able to pull

# The Inner Life

down the building because "he his guide requested" to let him lean his arms on the two main pillars.

In Milton's other dramatic poems as well as in *Samson Agonistes*, a good deal of guiding of a literal sort is spoken of. Some of the guiding has to do with important events. Let me offer a handful of examples to suggest the recurrence of the idea.

In *Comus*, the Lady asks Comus for guidance when she is lost in the wood; after proclaiming the intimacy of his knowledge of every "dingle or bushy dell," he says, "I can conduct you, Lady, to a low / But loyal cottage, where you may be safe" (319-20). The consequences of this guidance are—like so many other examples in Milton—not what was promised, but instead lead to danger. Actually, it was the duty of the Attendant Spirit to give "safe convoy" to favored persons through "this advent'rous glade," but this time he was a little tardy, despite his ability to come "swift as the Sparkle of a glancing Star"; he gets his chance later, after Sabrina dissolves the spell, and says: "I shall be your faithful guide / Through this gloomy covert wide." Little need now, with all danger past.

The Lady, for her part, has general confidence that

> the Supreme good, t' whom all things ill
> Are but as slavish officers of vengeance,
> Would send a glist'ring Guardian, if need were,
> To keep my life and honor unassail'd. (217-20)

The Elder Brother independently feels likewise; he proclaims, in a fit of adolescent hyperbole, that chastity is so dear to Heaven

> That when a soul is found sincerely so,
> A thousand liveried Angels lackey her,
> Driving far off each thing of sin and guilt. (454-56)

In *Paradise Lost*, a variety of characters serve as guides. The best one is God. Immediately after Adam's creation, he falls asleep; God appears to him in a dream and says

> call'd by thee I come thy Guide

169

# John Milton

To the Garden of bliss, thy seat prepar'd.
So saying, by the hand he took me rais'd,
And over Fields and Waters, as in Air
Smooth sliding without step, last led me up
A woody Mountain. (VIII, 298-303)

He is shown the Garden of Eden, and he awakes to find his dream real. Then God appears in person as his guide:

> hee who was my Guide
> Up hither, from among the Trees appear'd,
> Presence Divine. (VIII, 312-14)

With rejoicing and awe, Adam falls in adoration at the feet of his guide.

The worst guide, of course, is Satan, who leads Eve to the forbidden tree. "If thou accept / My conduct," says Satan, "I can bring thee thither soon." "Lead then, said *Eve*" (IX, 629-31). He does, she follows his guidance, and the catastrophe ensues.

Among others who guide, Adam finds Michael to be absolutely reliable. When they are about to climb the hill to see the panorama of future history unfold, Adam gratefully says:

Ascend, I follow thee, safe Guide, the path
Thou lead'st me, and to the hand of Heav'n submit.
(XI, 371-72)

His confidence is well placed, and they proceed in safety. Adam still has a concern about the guidance of man in the distant future. After Christ returns to Heaven, what then, Adam asks Michael? "Who then shall guide / His people, who defend?" (XII, 482-83). Michael informs and comforts him about this part of the future as well.

In *Paradise Regained*, matters are far simpler. The question of who will be the guide arises very early in the poem, when Christ first meets Satan in the wilderness. Satan implicitly offers to guide Christ. The whole direction of the poem is set when Christ refuses that kind of guidance. "Who brought me hither / Will

# The Inner Life

bring me hence," he says, "no other Guide I seek" (I, 335-36). And no other guide does he turn to throughout the poem.

The figure of the guide is natural for a blind person, and it may be that Milton's blindness led him to think of the world, more than the sighted do, in terms of guides and guidance. Here are some of Milton's reflections (notice his use of the word "guidance" and the idea of being taken by the hand and led) on the subject in 1654, a couple of years after his blindness had become complete. He was writing to Leonard Philaras, who had offered to consult a famous oculist in Paris in search of the cause and cure of Milton's blindness:

> Why should one not likewise find comfort in believing that he cannot see by the eyes alone, but by the guidance and wisdom of God. Indeed while He himself looks out for me and provides for me, which He does, and takes me as if by the hand and leads me throughout life, surely, since it has pleased Him, I shall be pleased to grant my eyes a holiday. (*Prose*, IV, 870)

But the idea of guidance is also common in his writings before he lost his sight, and its recurrence can lead us on to a further inquiry. That is: if we stand in need of guidance, to what kinds of sources can we turn for help, and to what effect?

In the sections that follow, I would like, first, to explore Milton's own principles about the sources of guidance that are available to human beings, for the health of their inner life. Next, I would like to discuss some of the problems and difficulties with which Milton confronted his characters as they sought guidance in a world filled with deception. Then, the revelations that Milton offers about the guidance of his own inner life. And finally, the inner life of his leading characters in their search for guidance.

## I

For Milton, the sources of guidance were, in principle, beautifully simple. They consisted of nothing more, really, than Holy

# John Milton

Scripture and the Spirit of God. In practice, however, this kind of simplicity leads to exquisite complexity.

He could have taken a position much more easily than he did, I expect, if he had chosen any of the other three commonly accepted sources of guidance. He had rather little to say in favor of one of them, the Church, the bastion of earlier guidance, including the teachings and traditions of the Church and the Fathers of the Church. The two prime sources of modern guidance were not important to him for this purpose. I mean the State (including the code of law, the body of precedent, and the managers and adjudicators of the same) and the Community (including all social forces and contemporary customs, to the extent that they impinge on the individual).

For Milton, the primary and essential source of knowledge for man is Holy Scripture, so far as guidance for the most important aspect of his life is concerned. Throughout his life, Milton steeped himself in the Bible, and the full evidences of that learning are nowhere more visible than in his *Christian Doctrine*.

This massive book, in which Milton undertook to set forth all that is essential to Christian theology (including the nature of God and the nature of the Christian life), bears as its subtitle "Compiled from the Holy Scripture Alone." And so it was. Milton supports his own positions (which are stated briefly) with citations from Scripture (which are given very amply). Unlike his standard practice in polemical prose, he avoids citing commentators (or "learning"), and he did not go into theological disputes.

Milton repeatedly asserted the primacy of the Scripture. The study of Scripture, he said in *Considerations Touching the Likeliest Means to Remove Hirelings out of the Church*, "is the only true theologie" and that the gospel "is now the only dispensation of God to all men" (*Prose*, VII, 306, 277). His last word on this subject, in *Of True Religion*, was that, for all Protestant churches, the first main principle is that "the Rule of true Religion is the Word of God only" (*Works*, VI, 166).

Easier to say than to apply, as Milton well realized. His reason for insisting so strenuously on the primacy of the Scripture was to be sure that it was set above human learning or tradition or the teachings of a church. The adequate understanding of Scripture was a difficult task in Milton's view, as he was certainly not a fundamentalist in the modern sense of that term. God gave man the necessary ability to be able to understand Scripture, Milton felt; sometimes he called that ability *right reason*, and sometimes he called it *conscience*. In *Christian Doctrine*, he says that "Further evidence for the existence of God is provided by the phenomenon of Conscience, or right reason. This cannot be altogether asleep, even in the most evil men" (*Prose*, VI, 132).

Another way to put it is to say that conscience is man's connecting link with God. In *Paradise Lost*, God tells Christ that

> I will place within them [men] as a guide
> My Umpire *Conscience*, whom if they will hear,
> Light after light well us'd they shall attain,
> And to the end persisting, safe arrive. (III, 194-97)

Milton speaks on occasion of the operation of his own conscience. In Letter 5 (1633), he feels bound to explain his slow maturing, "according to the praecept of my conscience, w^ch I firmly trust is not w^thout god" (*Prose*, I, 319). And in *Reason of Church-Government*, he says that "if God by his Secretary conscience injoyn it, it were sad for me if I should draw back" (*Prose*, I, 822).

Conscience is our guide in the understanding of Scripture, but our conscience is our own personal, individual guide. My conscience cannot guide another, and the conscience of another cannot guide me. "No man, no synod, no session of men," wrote Milton in *Treatise of Civil Power*, "can judge definitively the sense of scripture to another mans conscience" (*Prose*, VII, 247-48).

Conscience or right reason is the perfect guide, ideally. But, as Michael explains to Adam, "Since thy original lapse, true Liberty / Is lost, which always with right Reason dwells / Twinn'd, and from her hath no dividual being." Thus it is that "reason in man" is "obscur'd, or not obey'd" (*PL*, XII, 83-86).

With this obscure prospect, we might well feel like joining Milton's groan in *Of Reformation*: "O Sir, I doe now feele my selfe in

# John Milton

wrapt on the sodaine into those mazes and *Labyrinths* of dreadfull and hideous thoughts, that which way to get out, or which way to end I know not." Unless, he goes on, "unlesse I turne mine eyes, and with your help lift up my hand to that Eternall and Propitious *Throne*, where nothing is readier than *grace* and *refuge* to the distresses of mortall Suppliants" (*Prose*, I, 613).

Fortunately, man does have this other source of guidance available to him, in addition to Scripture. He has the Spirit of God to guide him. Milton uses a number of different terms for this comforting idea. The Spirit of God most often, perhaps, but also the Holy Spirit, or the Comforter, or the mind of Christ in man, or Celestial Light, or inward light. Since it is not to my purpose to open up theological distinctions, I will not try to define exactly what manifestation or presence of God Milton means by these terms. The topic continues to be hotly disputed among specialists, but their differences do not affect my argument.

Milton felt, in principle, that every Christian had both the Scripture and the Spirit of God as his guides. "Every true Christian able to give a reason of his faith," he wrote in the *Treatise of Civil Power*, "hath the word of God before him, the promised Holy Spirit, and the minde of Christ within him." And when it comes to knowing how to receive opinions from Scripture, "to interpret convincingly to his own conscience none is able but himself guided by the Holy Spirit; and not so guided, none then he to himself can be a worse deceiver" (*Prose*, VII, 244, 249).

While Milton always looked toward the two sources of guidance, I believe that he gradually set a greater value on the Spirit of God within, on "that divine particle of Gods breathing, the soul" (as he referred to it early, in *Reason of Church-Government*, *Prose*, I, 848). When Adam asks Michael "Who then shall guide / His people, who defend?" Michael replies:

> from Heav'n
> Hee to his own a Comforter will send,
> The promise of the Father, who shall dwell
> His Spirit within them, and the Law of Faith
> Working through love, upon thir hearts shall write,

174

# The Inner Life

To guide them in all truth, and also arm
With spiritual Armor, able to resist
*Satan's* assaults, and quench his fiery darts.
(PL, XII, 482-92)

And in *Paradise Regained*, Milton has Christ say: "he who receives / Light from above, from the fountain of light, / No other doctrine needs" (IV, 288-90).

I believe that the increasing emphasis on the role of the Spirit of God within man had an important corollary for Milton. I believe that his poetry also became, at the same time, more inward in its feeling and in its mood and in its intent. In the major poems, Milton's preoccupation is with the inside, with the inner life.

It is only within this context of the role of the Spirit of God, I think, that we can fully appreciate Milton's invocations. I mentioned earlier the frequency with which he wrote them, and how superb he was as a master of the genre. We can see more of the richness of their real meaning for him if our eyes are fully open to what this form of guidance really meant to him. The appeal to the Holy Spirit in the invocation to Book I of *Paradise Lost* is made from an open heart:

> O Spirit, that dost prefer
> Before all Temples th' upright heart and pure,
> Instruct me, for Thou know'st; Thou from the first
> Wast present, and with mighty wings outspread
> Dove-like satst brooding on the vast Abyss
> And mad'st it pregnant: What in me is dark
> Illumine, what is low raise and support;
> That to the highth of this great Argument
> I may assert Eternal Providence,
> And justify the ways of God to men.

It is an intensely personal expression of need and an inner plea for help, offered to what he thought the essential source of guidance for man. Similarly, the conclusion to the invocation to Book III is a noble particular version of the same plea, to the same source of guidance:

> Celestial Light
> Shine inward, and the mind through all her powers
> Irradiate, there plant eyes, all mist from thence
> Purge and disperse, that I may see and tell
> Of things invisible to mortal sight.

Finally, the crux of the invocation in *Paradise Regained* is the same appeal yet once more: "Thou Spirit…inspire, / As thou art wont, my prompted Song, else mute."

## II

True principles do not necessarily solve all problems within their purview. The sources of guidance may be clear, but there can still be many practical difficulties in knowing how to get at them or follow them.

Milton chose to represent the worlds of his dramatic poems as filled with problems for the occupants of those worlds. I spoke in the last chapter about his preoccupation with a sense of struggle, conflict, and temptation. Behind that turmoil, however, lies a more basic issue. That is, the question of distinguishing true from false. Is it, for example, God's guidance or Satan's blandishment? How is the individual to know, on his own? In Milton's representations, it is not easy unless you are God.

The worlds of Milton's dramatic poems are teeming with difficulties of distinguishing–difficulties that Milton represents by the frequent use of disguise, by enchantment, by lies, and by deception of almost every conceivable sort. It is worth reviewing some examples of the different forms of deception that form the texture of the poems. I think that we appreciate the outlook of Milton and of his dramatic poems more fully when we see how extensively and how deeply the idea of deception permeates his poems.

Consider disguises. In *Comus*, the Lady first sees Comus in the disguise of a "gentle Shepherd," and she is completely taken in by him. Not all disguises have wicked intent, however. The Attendant Spirit appears to the brothers as their father's shepherd, Thyrsis, and of course they too are taken in. (It is only in the Epilogue that we learn that the Attendant Spirit / Thyrsis is really a creature that lives somewhere out there in fairyland.)

In *Paradise Lost*, Satan is truly the great master of disguises. He can be, as the occasion arises, a serpent, a toad, a lion, or a stripling cherub. Since his disguises are allowed to be good enough to deceive even the Archangel Uriel, it is hard to blame Eve or Adam for being misled. Satan also practises the art of character transformation and can take many roles, such as an orator, a general, a champion, an explorer, a diplomat, and a spy.

In *Paradise Regained*, Satan first appeared to Christ (very much as Comus had appeared to the Lady) as "an aged man in Rural weeds, / Following, as seem'd, the quest of some stray Ewe." Christ sees through the disguise almost right away "(For I discern thee other than thou seem'st)," and soon faces him down: "Why dost thou then suggest to me distrust, / Knowing who I am, as I know who thou art?" In his second appearance before Christ, Satan is in yet another disguise, "Not rustic as before, but seemlier clad, / As one in City, or Court, or Palace bred" (II, 299-300)—even though he knows he will be recognized.

In addition to disguises, the dramatic poems are full of enchantments, spells, charms, and other forms of magic. *Comus* is essentially a poem of enchantment. Comus has his charming rod, enchanted chair, "dazzling spells," the "power to cheat the eye," a magical cup, the art to recognize the different step made by a chaste foot, and the ability to turn human beings into beasts. The Attendant Spirit has the magical power of second sight, instant travel, and the herb haemony; he can also conjure. Sabrina, for her part, has the power (by an elaborate process) to undo spells.

The principal magician in both *Paradise Lost* and *Paradise Regained* is Satan; by comparison, all the others are small-time artists. Satan can take any form he chooses, appear and disappear at will, summon an instantaneous banquet, carry someone to a new

177

location in a flash, and perform all manner of other wonders. He is a little of a show-off in his performances, even with Christ; at the end of their first encounter, Satan bows "his gray dissimulation" low before Christ and then suddenly "disappear'd / Into thin Air diffus'd" (*PR*, I, 497-99). Milton allows even God to display what would in another be called magic, such as putting dreams into the heads of sleepers and whisking persons to a mountain top without taking a step.

In *Samson Agonistes*, Harapha claims that Samson couldn't have performed his feats without the use of spells, black enchantments, and the magician's art. For once, no magic was involved. Samson stiffly replies, "I know no spells, use no forbidden Arts; / My trust is in the living God who gave me / At my Nativity this strength" (1139-41). Harapha can be excused for his mistake.

There is an even more pervasive kind of deception throughout the dramatic poems, however. That is the deception of lies and other verbal dissimulation. All of the characters who are on the side of villainy are inveterate liars, and they shape facts and opinions to their own purposes. Satan–the Prince of Lies–speaks on behalf of this whole crowd (and for many others as well) when he says to Christ:

> where
> Easily canst thou find one miserable,
> And not enforc'd ofttimes to part from truth,
> If it may stand him more in stead to lie,
> Say and unsay, feign, flatter, or abjure? (*PR*, I, 470-74)

Satan's own tactics are to say whatever is best calculated to achieve his ends. In the encounter with Sin and Death, for example, Satan angrily replies to Sin as follows before he knows what they can do for him:

> What thing thou art, thus double-form'd, and why
> In this infernal Vale first met thou call'st
> Me Father, and that Phantasm call'st my Son?
> I know thee not, nor ever saw till now

# The Inner Life

Sight more detestable than him and thee.

(PL, II, 741-45)

As soon as he realizes that he needs their favor to get out of Hell, he changes his tune to this smooth address to them:

> Dear Daughter, since thou claim'st me for thy Sire,
> And my fair Son here shows't me, the dear pledge
> Of dalliance had with thee in Heav'n. (II, 817-19)

The lies of flattery succeed, and out he goes.

Satan can speak one way—and speak with glorious eloquence—while he actually feels quite another way. He delivers a fiery speech to Beelzebub with rousing enthusiasm:

> All is not lost; the unconquerable Will,
> And study of revenge, immortal hate,
> And courage never to submit or yield. (PL, I, 106-08)

His rhetoric would rattle the walls if there were any. Yet he delivers this message of hope, "Vaunting aloud, but rackt with deep despair" (I, 126).

You may sometimes feel that you hardly know what to believe in the dramatic poems. Dalila comes in the guise of a penitent, and there is no break in the surface of her sincerity. We finally become aware, aided by the symbolic tags of serpent and sorceress attached to her, of her hypocrisy. Even the motives of old Manoa, it turns out, are a bit on the shaky side in his claim that he wants to get Samson released to bring an end to the punishment, when his hope is actually a little more selfish. Even the Attendant Spirit in Comus is (I regret to say) not above a little deception in all that story he spins out to the two brothers about having been off tending the flocks; but at least he has no selfish motive in his modest fabrication.

The truth is that the world of Milton's dramatic poems is full of deception. *Paradise Lost* has, I believe, more deception in it than does any other important long poem in English. And Milton's other dramatic poems do not come far behind.

What does all this deception signify? It signifies, I believe, one important way in which Milton looked at the world. It signifies a world in which we have to tread cautiously, watch carefully, and observe closely. No matter. The world is still a tricky place. There is guidance for us, to be sure. But there is also false guidance everywhere, with the effort to lead us astray. And it is not easy to know which is which.

## III

These problems all bear down on the single, individual human being. It is he or she alone who must choose the guide, settle on principles, and find the way through a world of difficulties. In the world as Milton perceives it, there was certainly plenty of need for guidance.

Milton felt that he had himself received much guidance from God. He speaks, in the *Doctrine and Discipline of Divorce*, of the "unerring guidance" he has received "through the help of that illuminating Spirit which hath favor'd me" (*Prose*, II, 340). In the *Second Defence*, he said of God that "I know and recognize in the most momentous affairs his fatherly mercy and kindness towards me, and especially in this fact, that with his consolation strengthening my spirit I bow to his divine will" (*Prose*, IV, 589). To us ordinary, unilluminated people, Milton's remarks may sound so self-confident as to be arrogant. But what we might require to qualify it as modesty would cloak a simple statement of his belief in a false garment of rhetoric, and Milton is trying to speak in absolute honesty. He goes on, in the *Second Defence*, to express his sense of God's special favor toward him as a blind man:

> We blind men are not the least of God's concerns, for the less able we are to perceive anything other than himself, the more mercifully and graciously does he deign to look upon us. Woe to him who mocks us, woe to him who injures us. He deserves to be cursed with a public malediction. Divine law and divine favor have rendered us not only safe from the injuries of men, but almost sacred, nor do these shadows around us seem to have been created so much by the dull-

ness of our eyes as by the shade of angels' wings. And divine favor not infrequently is wont to lighten these shadows again, once made, by an inner and far more enduring light. (*Prose*, IV, 590)

I believe that Milton's invocations to God in his poetry are much more understandable when they are read in the light of this sense of his own certainty. He felt that he *did* have special favor from God, that he *was* given special illumination by God, and that he *did* have the inner light from God. Hence it was only proper for him to seek God's guidance and help when he felt that he needed it. It is perfectly understandable that he should think he needed help when he was writing poetry, as writing poetry was a mission of vast importance to him. And it is perfectly understandable that he should seek that help from God, since God was his constant guide.

Being the recipient of special guidance from God was not always a special delight, however. In *Reason of Church-Government*, Milton speaks with sympathy of the burden that the ancient prophets felt because of being inspired by God. "Although divine inspiration must certainly have been sweet to those ancient profets, yet the irksomenesse of that truth which they brought was so unpleasant to them, that every where they call it a burden." And he is speaking for himself as well, apparently, when he goes on to say: "But when God commands to take the trumpet and blow a dolorous or a jarring blast, it lies not in mans will what he shall say, or what he shall conceal" (*Prose*, I, 802-03).

Milton left one solemn account, in the *Second Defence*, of his parleyings with the Almighty. It is such a rare and remarkable revelation of Milton's inner life that it deserves to be quoted once more. He is responding to the charge that his blindness was a punishment for his political writings, and his answer includes an account of his relations to God as guide:

> For my part, I call upon Thee, my God, who knowest my inmost mind and all my thoughts, to witness that (although I have repeatedly examined myself on this point as earnestly

181

# John Milton

as I could, and have searched all the corners of my life) I am conscious of nothing, or of no deed, either recent or remote, whose wickedness could justly occasion or invite upon me this supreme misfortune. As for what I have at any time written (since the royalists think that I am now undergoing this suffering as a penance, and they accordingly rejoice), I likewise call God to witness that I have written nothing of such kind that I was not then and am not now convinced that it was right and true and pleasing to God.... When the business of replying to the royal defense had been officially assigned to me, and at that same time I was afflicted at once by ill health and the virtual loss of my remaining eye, and the doctors were making learned predictions that if I should undertake this task, I would shortly lose both eyes, I was not in the least deterred by the warning. I seemed to hear, not the voice of the doctor (even that of Aesculapius, issuing from the shrine at Epidaurus), but the sound of a certain more divine monitor within. (*Prose*, IV, 587-88)

The account is rich in the sense of a close relation with God: the naturalness of calling on God as a witness, the conviction that his work is "pleasing to God," and following the guidance of that "divine monitor within."

There is an interesting parallel to Milton's own sense of guidance in Christ's meditation in the wilderness (*Paradise Regained*, I, 196-293). It, too, is a self-revelation under threatening circumstances and surrounded by darkness. Christ is alone with "his deep thoughts," with "the Spirit leading" him. He is trying to sort out his own sense of himself and to compare that with the sense that others express about him:

O what a multitude of thoughts at once
Awak'n'd in me swarm, while I consider
What from within I feel myself, and hear
What from without comes often to my ears.

It is that inner life with which he wants to come to terms. He reviews his childhood, play, learning; he thinks of himself as having been a serious child, devoted to a mission of public good for which he felt destined. He received guidance from his mother, who told him how the shepherds were "directed to the Manger" and how the new star "guided the Wise Men." He studied "the Law and Prophets" (the equivalent of Milton's Scripture) to learn about the Messiah, "and soon found of whom they speak / I am." After John the Baptist had been sent from God as his harbinger, the Spirit of God descended on him like a dove, and God spoke aloud to the world acknowledging him as the Son of God. He is aware that his authority is derived from God, and he concluded his meditation by saying:

> And now by some strong motion I am led
> Into this Wilderness, to what intent
> I learn not yet; perhaps I need not know;
> For what concerns my knowledge God reveals.

Christ's meditation parallels on the ideal level the principles of guidance that Milton expressed on the human level. There is the feeling of mission and the drive to live up to the needs of that mission. There is the recognition of Scripture as a primary source of knowledge from without for guidance. There is awareness of the presence of the Spirit of God as a source from within for guidance. There are the inner promptings from God ("some strong motion") with specific guidance which the faithful one follows without necessarily knowing the intention or the result, even though it may involve danger or death.

## IV

In the light of these thoughts on the inner life and guidance, I would like to conclude with some reflections about the inner life of several of the leading characters in Milton's principal poems, and the sense of guidance that each one of them has. I will speak first of Satan, then of Adam and Eve, and finally of Samson.

I believe that we know Satan more intimately than we do any other character in Milton's poetry. It could have been otherwise: he is perhaps Milton's most complex character, and there are

# John Milton

wide divergences between his secret intentions and his public utterances. We know Satan well because Milton causes these divergences to be revealed to us. Satan reveals himself in asides and soliloquies, and the omniscient characters keep us well informed as to his real motives and drives. So we are never deceived by appearances, no matter what he says or does in order to persuade others to take the course of action that will serve his darker design.

We are told over and over again about Satan's ruling passions. It was pride (or envy of God) that caused him to revolt. It was the desire for revenge against God and envy of others in a happier state that drove him to tempt Eve and Christ. In addition, malice made him seek companions for his eternal misery.

Satan is not always resolute, however. He has moments of uncertainty when he too undergoes temptation. His, ironically, is a temptation in reverse—that of giving up his pride and envy and malice, and of being guided in the direction of virtue and innocence and beauty.

When Satan first sees Adam and Eve, he is filled with wonder at their divine resemblance and "could love" them; but his desire for revenge overcomes the feeling that made him "melt" at their "harmless innocence," and he proceeds with his "devilish deeds" (IV, 358-92).

When he first sees the earth, he is tempted to have "delight" and "joy" in walking around and enjoying its beauty; but the thought of pleasure brings him torment:

> the more I see
> Pleasures about me, so much more I feel
> Torment within me, as from the hateful siege
> Of contraries; all good to me becomes
> Bane.

He recovers from the temptation, "For only in destroying I find ease / To my relentless thoughts" (IX, 99-130).

When Satan first sees Eve, her beauty overawed

> His Malice, and with rapine sweet bereav'd

# The Inner Life

His fierceness of the fierce intent it brought:
That space the Evil one abstracted stood
From his own evil, and for the time remain'd
Stupidly good, of enmity disarm'd
Of guile, of hate, of envy, of revenge.

He soon recovers, however; "Fierce hate he recollects, and all his thoughts / Of mischief, gratulating, thus excites" and he speaks in favor of "hate, not love," in favor of "pleasure to destroy" rather than "to taste of pleasure" (IX, 452-79).

Despair is often near the surface of his feelings. When he first approaches Eden, "he falls," as the Argument to Book IV tells us, "into many doubts with himself, and many passions, fear, envy, and despair." The poem itself reports the attack of his passions, as "horror and doubt distract / His troubl'd thoughts"; he still has conscience within him, and "conscience wakes despair / That slumber'd"—though never for long, as despair is always ready to rouse up and beset him.

From the reports of Satan's inner life, we come to recognize what his sources of guidance are. They are nothing like the ones that Milton recommended. They are all within himself, and all of them are his passions. In time of uncertainty, or doubt, or despair, he turns to those passions—of envy and hatred and the rest—and they guide him and give him courage to persist in the ways of malice and wickedness.

Still, we sometimes sympathize with Satan. Perhaps because we have been made aware of his inner life and know something of his real feelings. For many of us, there is a touch of secret sympathy for Satan for some reason that is peculiar to our personal needs, such as that he is the underdog, or that he may not be getting a fair deal, or that he is bold and energetic. This may be like the secret harmony with Satan that was felt by Sin, who could divine his success because her "Heart, which by a secret harmony, / Still moves with thine, join'd in connexion sweet" (X, 358-59). Our "secret harmony" is (we should confess) likely to be more with Satan than with any of the other characters, if the

185

# John Milton

poem can succeed in revealing something of the inner life of the reader as well as its own character. We are doubtless, for the most part, not members of the Devil's party without knowing it, but we might on occasion give him our vote in a really secret ballot.

The inner feelings of Adam and Eve are also revealed to us, though mostly by themselves. A brief reminder of what they do after the fall can focus our attention on the shifts that take place in their guidance. Upon waking from the sleep that followed their extended "amorous play," Adam observes "the signs / Of foul concupiscence," he is overcome by shame, and he wishes that he could hide away in a solitary, savage life or (at last) that their nakedness could at least be covered up (IX, 1067-1120). They begin to weep, their reason is replaced by passion, and each one bitterly condemns the other for their unhappy plight (IX, 1120-89). Adam falls into a state of deep despair: he lies outstretched on the cold ground, terrified by his "evil Conscience"; he curses his creation, wishes for death, and repudiates Eve (X, 845-908).

Adam is indeed at his lowest point. Then the inner movement shifts, and it does so because of the actions of Eve. She had guided Adam into sin, and now, unwittingly, she is the guide once more as she leads him out of the depths of despair. She does so by begging his forgiveness, by weeping, by taking the blame on herself, and by falling at his feet in submission (X, 909-36). (It is a model example of natural therapy.) Adam relents in his passionate feeling against her, forgives her, and offers to take the blame on himself instead (X, 937-65). Eve, in a spirit of self-abasement and sacrifice, suggests childlessness or suicide (X, 966-1006). Adam turns their course of action toward penitence to God and toward seeking instruction from him. They join in confessing their faults and in begging for pardon, with "hearts contrite, in sign / Of sorrow unfeign'd, and humiliation meek" (X, 1007-1104).

They have done all they can do in changing their guidance from themselves to the will of God, and Book X concludes. Book XI then begins: "Thus they in lowliest plight repentant stood /

# The Inner Life

Praying." They were able to do this because the Spirit of God had descended on them and

>                                           had remov'd
> The stony from thir hearts, and made new flesh
> Regenerate grow instead, that sighs now breath'd
> Unutterable, which the Spirit of prayer
> Inspir'd. (X, 3-7)

Milton makes it very clear that it is the Spirit of God that is at work in Adam and Eve. God himself observes about Adam that

> He sorrows now, repents, and prays contrite
> My motions in him; longer than they move,
> His heart I know, how variable and vain
> Self-left. (XI, 90-93)

"My motions in him," says God in this elliptical commentary on man's need for God's continuing guidance. Inspired by "the Spirit." Grace having "remov'd / The stony from thir hearts." Thus their guidance is once again in the hands of God.

It is worth noticing what a central role despair plays in the inner life of Milton's leading characters. It seems to be a special risk, of the gravest consequence, that Milton portrayed as evidence of the deepest kind of trouble. So it was with Satan, and with Adam and Eve. And so it is with Samson.

Throughout *Samson Agonistes*, Samson lives on the edge of that precipice of despair. His actions are altogether resolute, but he reveals a terrible, terrifying irresolution within his inner life.

His descriptions of his dejection are absolute classics of their kind:

> So much I feel my genial spirits droop,
> My hopes all flat, nature within me seems
> In all her functions weary of herself;
> My race of glory run, and race of shame,
> And I shall shortly be with them that rest. (594-98)

Manoa feels that this dejection proceeds from "anguish of the

# John Milton

mind and humors black, / That mingle with thy fancy"—which is
an explanation that doesn't explain very much, but it supports
Manoa's conventional outlook. Samson longs (with everyone who
has ever suffered acute depression) for his torment to be confined
to his body; he yearns to get by with having sores all over himself
or with any combination of any other physical maladies. Anything else, he feels. Anything rather than let this torment

> secret passage find
> To th' inmost mind,
> There exercise all his fierce accidents,
> And on her purest spirits prey. (610-13)

But the torment has already lodged there, and he is in such des-
peration that he can look on "death's benumbing Opium as my
only cure." The root of his problem is that he is uncertain about
his guidance. He is not sure, but he has a "sense of Heav'ns desertion" (630-33).

Samson, like Adam and Eve, was tempted and fell. They were
tempted by Satan and disobeyed God by eating the fruit of the
forbidden tree; he was tempted by Dalila and disobeyed God by
revealing the secret source of his God-given strength. They felt
despair, acted to place themselves in submission to God, and regained the guidance of God; he felt despair, has been resolute in
acting according to his own guidance, and is now uncertain about
his relation with God. But it is still in the middle of things for
Samson, though it seems to him the end.

Earlier in his life, Samson had acted on inner promptings
which he received from God. In musing about his first marriage,
with the woman of Timna, Samson tells the Chorus that she
didn't please his parents because she was the daughter of an
infidel. But, he says:

> they knew not
> That what I motion'd was of God; I knew
> From intimate impulse, and therefore urg'd
> The Marriage on; that by occasion hence
> I might begin *Israel's* Deliverance,

188

# The Inner Life

The work to which I was divinely call'd. (221-26)

When she proved false, he goes on, he then married Dalila: "I thought it lawful from my former act, / And the same end; still watching to oppress / *Israel's* oppressors" (231-33). Manoa later confirms that he hadn't approved Samson's two marriage choices, "but thou didst plead / Divine impulsion prompting" how he might be able to overcome the foes of Israel (421-23).

Apparently Samson has not felt any inner promptings from God since he was tempted and broke his vow of silence. Neither had he received any other sign of the presence of the Spirit of God. All of these matters need to be kept in mind as the end of the poem approaches. The Messenger comes with the demand of the Philistine Lords. To Samson, the demand seems like another temptation to test his strength of character. He consults his own thoughts. All reason is against acceding to the demand, and he declines the order, with resolution and contempt, despite the worldly urgings of those around him.

Then, all of a sudden comes the inner prompting! Samson has just answered the arguments of the Chorus that he should go. But when God's prompting comes, Samson does not even consider making an answer. He simply obeys, instantly:

> I begin to feel
> Some rousing motions in me which dispose
> To something extraordinary my thoughts.

Just that, and nothing more. Nothing more is needed. Samson is already resolved:

> I with this Messenger will go along,
> Nothing to do, be sure, that may dishonor
> Our Law, or stain my vow of *Nazarite*.
> If there be aught of presage in the mind,
> This day will be remarkable in my life
> By some great act, or of my days the last. (1381-89)

He doesn't know what the prompting means, and he doesn't

know what the consequences will be. But he knows its source, and that is enough for him.

Samson's obedience to the prompting is the equivalent of the contrition of Adam and Eve and their submission to the will of God. What the judgment on Samson will be we do not know. We do know that he is back under the right guidance.

In the concluding reflections of the poem, we should take special notice of the Semichorus's crucial comment that Samson proceeded to his task "With inward eyes illuminated / His fiery virtue rous'd" (1689-90). Also, old Manoa is given the honor of making the reiteration that Samson acted under the guidance of God and was reunited with him:

> And which is best and happiest yet, all this
> With God not parted from him, as was fear'd,
> But favoring and assisting to the end.
> Nothing is here for tears, nothing to wail
> Or knock the breast. (1718-22)

The final word is by the Chorus, and it brings to a peaceful close all those doubts that had troubled Samson and had left him in a state of utter despair:

> All is best, though we oft doubt,
> What th' unsearchable dispose
> Of highest wisdom brings about,
> And ever best found in the close. (1745-48)

This kind of peace, which is ever best, can be attained only by being in tune with the voice of highest wisdom whenever it speaks.

For Samson, for Adam and Eve, and for Satan, it was the inner life that counted for the most, so far as Milton was concerned. And so it was also with Milton himself. Within him, we can perceive flashes of those ideas that animated his poems. Within his poems, we can see, as in distant mirrors, reflections of Milton's governing ideas.

# The Inner Life

That world within is man's most precious part, his greatest treasure. It needs and deserves the best guidance it can get. The inner life is the place of final truth.